WRITE
WHAT'S
WRONG

WRITE WHAT'S WRONG

Using Handwriting to Reveal Hidden Health Problems

CLAUDE SANTOY, PH.D.

PARAGON HOUSE

NEW YORK

First Edition, 1992

Published in the United States by
Paragon House
90 Fifth Avenue
New York, N.Y. 10011

Copyright © 1992 by Paragon House Publishers

Editorial development by Barbara Brooks

Manufactured in the United States of America

Library of Congress Cataloging-in-Publication Data

Santoy, Claude.
    Write what's wrong : using handwriting to reveal hidden health
problems / Claude Santoy. —1st ed.
        p.   cm.
    ISBN 1-55778-339-X (alk. paper) : $10.95
    1. Graphology—Diagnostic use.   I. Title.
BF905.M43S26   1992
155.2′82—dc20   91-21221
                                                          CIP

The paper used in this publication meets the minimum requirements of American National Standard for Information Sciences—Permanence of Paper for Printed Library Materials, ANSI Z39.48-1984.

CONTENTS

2

IDENTIFYING PROBLEMS

---------- 3 ----------

PHYSICAL ILLNESS

---------- 4 ----------

PSYCHOLOGICAL WELL-BEING

5

TESTING YOUR SKILL

INTRODUCTION

How well do you *really* know your partner? Are your business associates honest? Does a loved one suffer from a physical condition or illness neither of you knows about? *Write What's Wrong* can help you find out.

You can learn how to analyze and interpret handwriting with any of my books. It's cheaper than hiring a private detective to find out whether your lover is honest. It's more accurate as a hiring criterion than the Personnel Department's battery of psychological tests. It can even be adapted as a therapeutic tool.

Graphology is not magic. It is a science, based on observation. A person's handwriting reveals the current state of body and mind. Indeed, all graphic expression mirrors thought, emotion, and health. If your heart beats irregularly because you have a cardiovascular problem, your writing strokes automatically reflect your condition, most often as a shaky (spasmodic) pressure on the page or as breaks in the strokes of individual letters. General mental instability may show up either in a too-perfect, monotonous-looking script or in wavy lines of writing that meander across the page. Victims of schizophrenia often underscore pieces or entire passages of their handwriting samples.

Whether you're 8 or 80, your physical and mental predispositions show up in your handwriting. That's why businesses, governments, and individuals around the world rely on graphology as a basic element in their decision making—from analyzing applicants' aptitudes for careers or specific jobs, their personality traits, the compatability of one person with another, their trustworthiness and even a person's state of physical and mental health.

Graphology is based on observation and practiced by analogy. Pioneers in handwriting analysis developed their methods by observing and interpreting a wide variety of samples. They laid the base for anyone to acquire the skill.

My method for handwriting analysis will teach you to distinguish more than just tendencies or predispositions. As you learn the technique and proceed by analogy through the more than 150 samples in this book—samples gathered from a wide variety of people in many countries—you'll quickly begin to apply your new skill. And you'll use graphology in your business and in your personal and professional life. You'll see right away the many kinds of useful information handwriting analysis yields to the practiced eye. It's fascinating, and it's fun.

Read on, and enjoy.

1

INITIATION

Throw out all your notions about "good" and "bad" handwriting. The first thing you should know is this: What's generally accepted as a "beautiful hand" has no meaning for the graphologist. It all depends on the age, sex, and profession of the writer, *and* on the situation.

In handwriting analysis, one isolated stroke or shape may have several meanings. As you analyze the individual elements of a handwriting sample—the size, slant, shape, pressure, and speed of the script—you will draw your interpretation from the whole. It's the interplay and accumulation of all elements together that signal probable traits or behaviors that are pronounced in the writer relative to other people. Likewise, prominent, frequently recurring elements signal specific aspects of physical or mental health.

Consider lying. While some of us are better at it than others, we all tell fibs out of politeness, tact, or to be diplomatic, and any of these traits may show up in our handwriting, as may one or two of the many graphical signs of lying. *But*, the more numerous the individual signs for lying, the more reliable the interpretation of the writer as someone whose lying has crossed the line from politeness or tact into deceit or even compulsive lying. You will learn several sig-

1

nals of lying in the Glossary of Traits at the end of this chapter.

Be assured, it's easier to disguise the meaning of your words than it is to disguise the meaning of your handwriting strokes. Graphology reveals the writer's inner aspects—aspects often inconsistent with outward physical appearance and sometimes even with behavior. So even though it's easier to profile the mental state of a person than to pinpoint a physical ailment, graphology is a valuable complement both to medicine and to psychology. Any background you have in either of these fields will help your exploration here.

HOW TO CHOOSE SAMPLES

The best way to learn graphology is to collect samples, at first from friends you know and later from others, whom you'll get to know through their handwriting. Samples should be written in ballpoint or fountain pen on unlined white paper. Avoid photocopies, felt markers, and soft-tip pens, which make it impossible to detect the pressure of the strokes and therefore to assess the general physical health of the writer.

The ideal sample is a spontaneous message of several lines, written to you personally. Make a note of the writer's age, sex, and profession or have the writer include this information. Content is not important, but the message should be the writer's original thoughts. Copying a poem or other passage or writing from dictation tend to make the handwriting mechanical and likely will distort your analysis.

In fact, you need not know the language used in the sample, as long as it's the writer's native tongue and the message is spontaneous. But note too that my method is based on written languages that read from left to right and from the top to the bottom of the page. For this reason, you cannot use it to analyze samples written in Middle Eastern or Oriental languages, however, Russian and Greek can be analysed.

TOOLS

You don't need much equipment. Just gather up a ruler, a protractor, and a magnifying glass. You'll measure the size of letters, the spacing between words, and the slope of the lines of writing with the ruler. The protractor shows the slant of the strokes. The magnifier lets you see details.

Developing the skill you'll need to venture an interpretation is simply a matter of familiarizing yourself with the basics that follow and then proceeding by analogy through the many handwriting samples that comprise the book. People are complex. Psychologists tell us that, along with our physical, genetic makeup, each of us has inborn mental and emotional predispositions—a temperament—that combine with early childhood experiences to foreshadow our adult states of body and mind. Any character trait or predisposition can have positive or negative effects, depending on the individual's inherited reaction pattern and on the situation.

So your primary tool is your own attitude toward interpreting handwriting. Remain flexible and open minded. People are as individual as their handwriting styles. They go through physical and psychological changes. The same person may be easily influenced or stubborn, moody or even-tempered, shy or aggressive, depending on the situation.

EVALUATING THE LAYOUT OF A SAMPLE

The most basic element to analyze is the overall layout of the sample—the margins, spacing, signature, and even the address on the envelope. Apply the following guidelines and diagrams on general layout aspects to any samples you collect. Compare your handwriting samples with the examples of script that accompany descriptions of specific aspects.

Margins

One of the easiest aspects to interpret in isolation, margins alone don't tell the tale. Your first impression may feel absolute, but you'll more often than not change it as you accumulate information. As always, it will blend with your other discoveries.

For comparison, take a look at the margins in these four diagrams. Detail on these and other significant aspects of margins follows. Here, simply note the patterns: Beginning at the left, a generally positive aspect; second, the left margin decreases toward the bottom of the page; third, the left margin increases toward the bottom; fourth, the right margin is absent *and* the lines of writing slope downward.

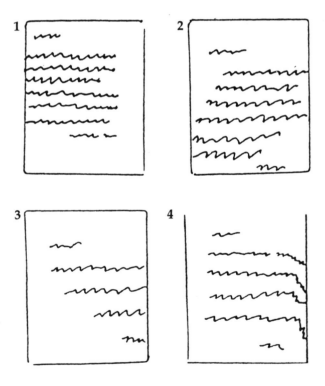

Margins are absent

When the entire page is filled with writing, your subject may exhibit selfishness, immaturity, bad judgment, or in the extreme, emotional instability.

Left margin is

Absent: Selfishness, lack of maturity.

Decreasing toward bottom: Caution or fear, weakness, pessimism, depression (see preceding diagram 2).

Extremely large: Fantasizing; psychological disorder.

Increasing toward bottom: Spontaneity, independence, carelessness; an easily influenced person (see diagram 3).

Irregular: Unstable or unreliable.

Wide and straight: Focused mind; considerate person (see diagram 1).

Right margin is

Absent or narrow: A vital, well-balanced person.

Absent with downward-sloping lines: Reckless, impatient, glib, or talkative (see diagram 4).

Large or irregular: Timid, fearful, inhibited, unstable.

Top margin is

Absent: Selfish or greedy, arrogant, immature.

Large: Humble; considerate.

* * *

Paragraphing

If the first line of each paragraph is indented, chances are the writer is an orderly, well-balanced person. Taking the time to indent paragraphs is as well a sign of consideration for the reader. If the first line of each paragraph begins at the left margin, the writer may be shy, inhibited, or immature.

* * *

Spacing

When you examine a handwriting sample you must consider the spacing between lines, words, and letters. The following characteristics apply:

Irregular spacing between letters and words reveals neurotic tendencies.

* * *

Lack of spacing between words and letters and entangled lines of script reveal psychological problems.

Narrow spacing between words and lines shows that the writer is selfish or avaricious.

* * *

Regular, even spacing between letters, words, and lines indicates a basically healthy, sociable person.

It occurs to me that
might be locating copies
ably's novels as you
- to England. Would
able / willing to

* * *

Wide spacing between words and lines hints at loneliness.

n have I see you
I day and dream
how it could be .....
is the secret of that

* * *

The Signature

A message without a signature yields less insight into the writer's personality than a signed sample. Conversely, a signature alone is insufficient to draw a clear, precise portrait. Your analysis of the signature is part of your study of the whole sample and follows, in general, the guidelines you'll use to interpret any handwriting.

REMEMBER: The most positive signature—and the most difficult to forge—is one that matches in every aspect the handwriting in the text of the sample. If the signature differs greatly from the handwriting of the text, your subject likely is not trustworthy. (Make exceptions for business executives or professionals who sign their names countless times each day. Here simplified or illegible signatures have no special meaning.)

The following are general guidelines for signatures and their relationship to the text of the message:

Paraphs

A paraph is a flourish or embellishment of the signature. Like their writers, paraphs come in all shapes and sizes:

*   *   *

If the signature is:

Crossed out with a paraph through its middle, as in the first example, the person may be vengeful or self-destructive.

Straight, horizontal paraphs under, over, or atop the signature are a sign of ambition, dynamism, and/or unconventional attitude.

Surrounded by a paraph, as in the middle example, this writer is attached to family and to material possessions.

Vertical paraphs, with strokes plunging downward (see example on the right) reveal a pragmatic person who may be capable of ruthlessness or selfishness. The writer likely has a good business sense and may be rather materialistic.

Size

If the signature is much larger or much smaller than the text of the message, chances are the writer is concealing feelings of inferiority. The smaller the signature (relative to the surrounding script) the stronger the feelings. Larger signatures indicate that the writer is channeling off these inner feelings as arrogant or vain behavior. (Note that very high stems or loops in the signature also reveal vanity. See the Glossary of Strokes coming up.)

Envelope Addresses

Knowing that you can generalize what you've learned about margins, spacing, and signatures to how the envelope is addressed, you may already have guessed that the more its script looks like the message the more positive the general interpretation. If the script on the envelope is dissimilar, the writer may be untrustworthy.

Of course, different address styles predominate in different countries. In the USSR, for instance, the address normally is written in the upper left. Barring cultural differences, the following guidelines apply:

If the address appears:

Slightly toward the lower right, the writer is an organized, well-balanced person.

At the lower right corner, the writer is ambitious, materialistic, and selfish.

In the upper left corner, the writer may be passive or inhibited, pessimistic, or intellectually frustrated.

In the lower left corner, the writer may be timid, vindictive, or sexually frustrated or inhibited.

Indented toward the right, reminding you of stair steps, the writer has a rough time trusting others and may in fact be untrustworthy. Unnecessary periods at the ends of lines intensify this interpretation.

To use the entire space, leaving no margins, the writer may display a strong or invasive personality and may be selfish and immature.

Scattered or irregular—a sign of a confused mind—the writer probably has psychological problems.

THE BASELINE

When you place your ruler beneath the lines of a writing sample, you will find the baseline. Get a general feel from your samples whether their baselines are wavy or irregular or generally move straight across the page. Does the baseline rise or fall? You'll find more specifics on the baseline as you peruse the Glossary of Strokes.

ZONES

Once you've developed an eye for the baseline you can begin identifying handwriting zones. The following sketch-plan shows the three principal zones and how they apply to overall predispositions or personality traits.

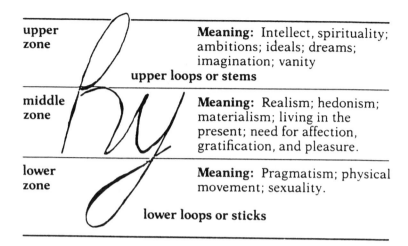

upper zone	**Meaning:** Intellect, spirituality; ambitions; ideals; dreams; imagination; vanity
	upper loops or stems
middle zone	**Meaning:** Realism; hedonism; materialism; living in the present; need for affection, gratification, and pleasure.
lower zone	**Meaning:** Pragmatism; physical movement; sexuality.
	lower loops or sticks

* * *

You'll find exaggerated activity in the upper zones of intellectual or spiritual people. Writing mainly in the middle zone might indicate a realist or perhaps an intensely materialistic person. Exaggerated activity in the lower zone reveals a pragmatic disposition and/or physical prowess. Pronounced loops in any zone may reveal deep-seated frustrations. Here are two examples.

Intellectual frustration:

Physical frustration:

* * *

SIZE

By itself, size is not a decisive element, but the size of script does offer general clues to broad character traits. You'll combine size with slant, shape, and pressure to round out your interpretations.

Large

Women and children usually writer larger than men. For your purposes, consider the handwriting large if capital letters measure a half inch or more in height and the lowercase letters stand around one-quarter inch or higher.

*   *   *

MEANING: Feminine, charming, creative, optimistic, vain, arrogant.

*   *   *

Medium

Capital letters measure one-quarter to one-half inch in height; lowercase letters are between one-ninth and one-fifth inch.

MEANING: In the absence of negative signs, a healthy, well-balanced person.

*   *   *

Small

Less than one-quarter-inch-high capitals; less than one-ninth-inch-high lowercase letters

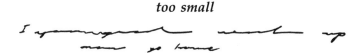

MEANING: Masculine, intelligent and/or well educated; a quick, alert mind.

* * *

Exaggerated

too small

MEANING: Anxious or fearful or impatient; humble or diplomatic; selfish or deceitful; greedy or egocentric; a person whose actions may be cut off from his or her emotions.

* * *

too large

MEANING: Immature, uneducated or unintelligent, grandiose, egocentric, vain, selfish.

SLANT

The slant is crucial, for it helps you to understand the writer's outlook (living in the past, present oriented, looking to the future); level of ambition; powers of concentration; and inhibitions.

THE PAST	THE PRESENT	THE FUTURE

MONOTONOUS (UPRIGHT)
SCRIPT:
Power of concentration
and reasoning;
discipline; economy;
tenacity.

BACKWARD (REVERSED) SLANT: Inhibitions, longing for or living in the past, repression and regret, pessimism, stubborness, deceit, dishonesty.

FORWARD (PROGRESSIVE) SLANT: Optimism, dynamism, enthusiasm, ambition, spontaneity, sociability, passion, anxiety, impatience.

BASELINE

Position your protractor on the baseline to gauge the slant of the script you're analyzing. Samples of these slants appear in the Glossary of Strokes. See the entries, *Baseline* and *Slant*.

Fluctuating Slant

Intense variation in the slant of words and/or in the slope of the baseline signals mental instability. This writer is prone to sudden, severe mood swings:

PRESSURE

In order to appraise pressure, hold the sample upside down and toward the light. If bulging lines appear, the pressure is heavy. If you can just barely guess that there is writing on the other side, the pressure is light. Pressure is difficult to judge in samples written in pencil or felt-tip pen. Above all, avoid trying to analyze photocopies!

The pressure of writing in a sample provides clues to many characteristics, foremost among them the relative health of the writer. By studying the samples throughout this book you will learn by analogy to evaluate pressure and to apply its specific meaning in your own samples. Beyond gauging physical health, pressure also may indicate:

- Mental balance
- Aggressive tendencies
- Energy level
- Need for affection
- Sensuality and strength of libido

Note that graphologists regard "libido" in an expanded sense. Beyond sexuality, the libido implies as well *joie de vivre* in a broad sense and entails basic aspects of the writer's attitude, outlook, and willpower.

> *Light pressure* can reflect cultural refinement, sensitivity, intelligence, a weak libido, precarious health.
> *Medium and heavy pressure* might signal robust health; a well-rounded, affectionate person; strong libido; intense frustration.
> *Shaky, or irregular pressure* usually is a danger signal and may reveal some combination of poor mental or physical health, emotional detachment, lack of self-control, or a problem with drugs or alcohol.

SPEED

Knowing the speed at which a person writes—in combination with your other observations—offers clues to overall disposition, integrity, intellect, and level of education. Like other individual signs, speed by itself has little meaning.

Speedy Writing

There are two ways to evaluate speed. The easiest is to watch your subject write. If this is not possible, remember that a sample written fast will show:

• A progressive slant
• Medium to light pressure
• Small- to medium-sized letters
• Round and/or simply-shaped letters
• Connected or a combination of connected and disconnected style of script.

Speedy writing is usually more positive than slow writing. It mainly reveals intelligence or a quick mind, honesty, sensitivity, impatience.

* * *

Slow Writing

Generally speaking, slow writing is never very positive. But take into consideration, for example, that young children, who are just learning to write, and adults who don't have much occasion to write may write slowly. Whether this is significant depends, as always, on the interplay of all your observations. Slow script tends to show:

- A regressive slant
- Unnecessary embellishments or alterations in letters
- Extreme angularity
- Heavy pressure
- Large-sized letters

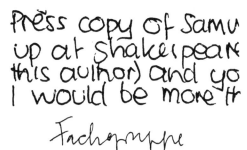

Slow writing might reveal creativity and manual dexterity, slow thinking, a lack of spontaneity or maturity, an unreliable or deceitful person.

WHAT SHAPES TELL US

Shape is the most fundamental aspect in handwriting analysis. At its most general level, the overall shape of a sample of script may impress you as round, angular, or a blend of the two. Children and women tend to use more round strokes; men's script tends to be angular.

Round script

Angular script

Each of us has both "masculine" and "feminine" traits—that is, traits that have come to be labeled as masculine or feminine by society. When we say that a handwriting sample reveals femininity or many masculine traits, we are referring to these cultural labels. The writer whose script we are analyzing might belong to either sex. The handwriting of a mature, well-balanced adult will contain a mixture of angular (masculine) and round (feminine) strokes.

TERMINOLOGY

There are few specific technical terms in graphology, and most of what there are will strike you as self-explanatory. Two alphabetical Glossaries follow—the Glossary of Strokes, complete with examples and meanings, followed by the Glossary of Traits, a selection of personality characteristics accompanied by the handwriting signs that define them. The Glossaries mirror one another. Put a bookmark here, for you will consult this section frequently as you cover the remaining chapters.

GLOSSARY OF STROKES

In the beginning you will refer often to this Glossary, but as you study more samples, you'll get a feel for each term and its corresponding stroke. Later on you will consult the Glossary only for exact meanings or shades of meaning. Often several meanings are given for one term, but all meanings do not apply in all cases. So flexibility is the watchword. In each handwriting sample there is an interplay of individual signs. Only in the context of the entire sample can you make your analysis or interpretation. An isolated sign gives no information. As your knowledge grows, your skills will improve, and you will learn to make the right choice among the possibilities.

*   *   *

Altered Strokes

The writer goes back to finished words or letters and tries to improve them, often for no reason. Shapes of letters may show a great variety of forms and are often difficult to recognize. You may need your magnifying glass to analyze the strokes.

MEANING: Perfectionism or obsessiveness; fear, anxiety; anguish; deceitfulness or hypocricy.

* * *

Angular Strokes

Sharp angles prevail.

MEANING: Virility; decisiveness, pragmatism, ambition; harshness, materialism, cruelty, selfishness, violence; inner tension. The writer is irascible and usually cannot be influenced. A principled person who is honest—unless the strokes show hooks and coils.

* * *

Arcades

Extremely rounded tops of letters; archlike links among letters, words, or other strokes; arches in capital letters. Often seen in *n* and *m*.

MEANING: Immaturity; vanity or arrogance; deceitfulness, manipulativeness, selfishness.

*   *   *

Backward Slant

Handwriting leans to the left. (Also called *reversed or sinistrogyric;* see *Slant.*)

with you - I would come tomorrow if I could but we plan for March!

MEANING: Immaturity, egocentricity, stubbornness; general lack of spontaneity; unresolved past problems, such as excessive attachment to the mother. This person can be deceitful as a friend and untrustworthy at work. Inner anxiety can prompt lying and "dissembling" or putting on a false face—that is, disguising or concealing facts, intentions, or feelings.

Left-handed writers, this applies as well to you! The writing slant of a normal, well-balanced lefty is progressive, leaning toward the right.

*   *   *

Baseline

When you place your ruler beneath the lines of a writing sample, you will find that the baseline may be straight, slightly meandering, or very meandering, and may ascend or descend on the page.

straight

handwriting

MEANING: Reliable, punctual, strong willpower; a principled person.

* * *

slightly meandering

taking up so much space.

MEANING: Lively; quick mind, intelligence; well-balanced character.

* * *

very meandering

golf tour for money. Written one chapbook of poetry, on

MEANING: Emotional instability; dishonesty or tendency to lie; mood swings. Could signal substance abuse and/or psychological problems.

* * *

ascendant

I make also a lot

MEANING: Optimism; dynamism, ambition; courage.

* * *

descendant

Whitman

MEANING: Pessimism, depression, poor health, illness.

* * *

Clubbed Strokes

Irregular pressure. Some strokes become thicker as the pressure increases. (See also *Spasmodic Script*.)

horizontal

To London until Sept. 1¢
here

MEANING: Emotional detachment; sexual ambivalence that is difficult to repress. Long, clubbed endstrokes reveal a tendency to push friends away brutally in order to preserve a sense of personal freedom.

* * *

vertical

George

MEANING: Sexual fantasizing; obsessiveness, inhibitions, frustrations; mental instability; drug or alcohol abuse.

* * *

Coils

Coils can appear in any letter, but you'll see them mainly in *a* and o and in the beginning and ending strokes of words.

MEANING: Positive aspects include business acumen, good concentration and reasoning power. Negative aspects include selfishness and dishonesty. The person lies and dissembles with ease. May indicate sexual perversion or immaturity.

* * *

Confused Script

Confusing to read because the writer uses the same basic shape for a great variety of letters.

MEANING: Emotional instability or psychological disorder; fear, anxiety, lack of trust; lying. The writer is unable to assume any responsiblities; fluctuating willpower.

* * *

Connected Script

MEANING: Analytical and deductive mind; mathematically gifted; good visual memory; sociable person.

* * *

Disconnected (Juxtaposed) Script

I saw Someone take fore me. Only when I home did I see the

talkative; great consideration for others; sometimes manual creativity.

*   *   *

Disconnected and Connected Script

Some letters inside words are connected and some are juxtaposed. Usually the person is a speedy writer.

have more to complain about !

MEANING: Intelligence; good education; intellectual creativity; quick mind.

*   *   *

Distorted Script

Twisted, strange strokes. Use your magnifying glass.

hand. I'm unable hand experience.

MEANING: Physical and mental pain, often involving glandular disorders.

*   *   *

Embellished Script

MEANING: Lack of education, intelligence, and/or maturity. The person is vain, childish, extremely selfish, and not trustworthy.

* * *

Garlands

The *m* and *n* are written like *u*, *v*, or *w*.

MEANING: Friendly, sociable, adaptable person who can be influenced easily.

* * *

Inhibited Script

Slow writing with tight spacing between letters, often accompanied by a backward slant.

MEANING: Inhibited, lacks spontaneity, egocentric, a selfish person who can dissemble and lie; good concentration.

* * *

Jumbled Script

Letters or lines flow into each other, making this handwriting difficult to read.

MEANING: Mental confusion, dishonesty, tendency toward psychological disorder. Denotes alcohol and/or drug abuse in advanced stages. Needs physical outlets.

* * *

Knotted Loops

Found in consonants; do not confuse with coiling strokes.

MEANING: Persistence, stubborness, tenacity, willpower, good concentration.

* * *

Launching Upward Strokes

MEANING: The writer has a violent temper and has difficulty keeping it in check. Aggressive, abusive behavior.

* * *

Overlapping Strokes

The writer goes over the same letter several times.

vacation

MEANING: Anxiety, emotional instability; lack of spontaneity; perseverance. Signals dishonesty (dissembling and lying) and/or sexual perversion.

* * *

Pasty Script

Thick, slow, heavy inkfilled strokes.

I dreamt about you people for the first time since I came to Europe one

MEANING: Cardiovascular problems; sloth; excessive and ambivalent sexual fantasies; sadistic tendencies; hidden aggressiveness.

* * *

Ringlets

Ringlets appear mainly in vowels and garland strokes.

eeeeee

MEANING: Charming, seductive, sociable, manipulative.

* * *

Round Strokes

Children and women use more round shapes, on the whole, than men.

you, but I'm very bar job is O.K., but I drink too much.

MEANING: Adaptable and sociable; may be easily influenced; immature.

* * *

Slant

forward (progressive)

to do because the grand

MEANING: Optimistic, ambitious, dynamic; passion for work and any chosen activity; spontaneity.

* * *

straight (upright)

Paris, but also to

MEANING: Good concentration; well-balanced, logical reasoning; ambitious, good memory.

* * *

backward (regressive or sinistrogyric)

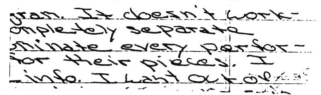

MEANING: Excessive attachment to the past and to unresolved problems which are yet to be overcome; egocentric, anxious; lack of spontaneity; immature, stubborn, deceitful, and dishonest.

* * *

Spasmodic Script (*See also* Clubbed Strokes)

Varying pressure within the strokes.

MEANING: Physical or mental illness; alcohol or drug abuse.

* * *

Sticklike Script

MEANING: Principled, yet rigid, behavior. May reveal cruelty; harsh, ruthless, selfish behavior; hard worker.

* * *

Tapered Strokes

Letters have a tapered or pointed finish; words may diminish in size.

MEANING: Destructive, caustic humor; cynical disposition. If the tapered stroke is vertical, indicates regressive libido.

* * *

Thread Letters and Connections

Script that looks like a continuous thread and is difficult to distinguish and to read.

MEANING: Positive aspects: diplomacy, good business acumen, intuition. On the negative side, often the person is untrustworthy and emotionally unstable—escapist, timid, inhibited, nervous, and impatient.

* * *

Unfinished Strokes

Letters do not reach the baseline.

MEANING: Timid, inhibited person who is sensitive, impressionable, and vulnerable. May be diplomatic, but inner anxiety prompts lying and dissembling. Indicates some degree of psychological distress.

GLOSSARY OF TRAITS

By reading through this first chapter you have acquired enough basic knowledge to begin analyzing handwriting. By training yourself to compare samples, you will begin to recognize specific character traits. If two people's scripts are never identical, they can be similar, and where they are, the meaning of the dominant traits will be the same and will be more pronounced in these people than in the population at large.

Physical pain and psychological suffering, whether prolonged or acute, can leave scars on the personality. The prominence of some traits can signal disorder, illness, or pain.

The Glossary of Traits broadens and applies what you've learned so far. As you read through the listing, note the handwriting signs that define various traits. Remember too that the sample strokes here represent extreme or pronounced examples of each trait in isolation. As always, when you compare any Glossary entry with a sample, you must keep in mind that your interpretation depends on the interplay of all elements, not on isolated strokes.

*   *   *

Aggression

Extreme aggression manifests itself in tapering, angular, and sticklike strokes; angular, knotted loops; and strong pressure.

*   *   *

Anger

Long, tapering strokes launching upward or downward through the lower zone; sinistrogyric strokes; and strong pressure all convey a sense of extreme anger.

* * *

Anxiety

Altered, covered strokes or letters; overlapping strokes; and sometimes, spasmodic pressure typify anxiety.

* * *

Arrogance

In many people, arrogant behavior results from an inferiority complex which the person cannot overcome.

Arcades appear in *n*, *m*, or capital letters and sometimes in the connections between two letters or words. You'll likely see these strokes in the signature or in the address too.

* * *

Asceticism

This person lives in extreme austerity like a hermit, refusing all communication with other people and all pleasures of life.

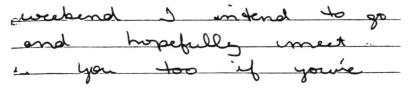

The handwriting sample will contain a sparse lower and middle zone, light pressure, very large spacing between words and lines, and disconnected or thread letters.

* * *

Callousness

A person who is hardened and lacks any kind of feelings for others.

Look for abrupt endings, upright slant, and sticklike strokes.

* * *

Cruelty

Strong pressure, sticklike strokes, tapering strokes, angular shapes, and angular sinistrogyric strokes appear in the sample. Vertical strokes reaching below the lower zone in the signature and vertical paraphs also signal a cruel nature.

* * *

Destructive and Self-Destructive Tendencies

Tapering, sometimes sinistrogyric strokes are among the signs, as is a crossed-out signature.

* * *

Egocentric Person

Egocentric behavior reveals itself in a slow, sinistrogyric script; tight letters; reduced spacing; and embellished or coiled letters. Sometimes there is a monotonous aspect in the handwriting.

* * *

Frustration

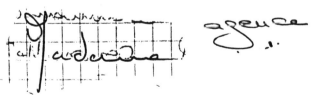

In general you will note a reduced middle zone with long upper or lower loops and stems. High upper stems show frustration in the achievement of higher goals. Very long lower loops show sexual and materialistic frustration. Prolonged or deep frustrations can produce emotional instability.

* * *

Greed

Abrupt endings; very small, tight letters; reduced spacing. Slow script with embellished letters, coils, sinistrogyric strokes.

* * *

Inhibition

The script displays a backward slant or strokes, tight spacing, slow writing, artificial shapes, coils, and overlapping strokes.

* * *

Instability

Extreme instability reveals neurosis.

Look for a very meandering baseline, light pressure, and discordant, confusing letters.

* * *

Jealousy

Knotted upper and lower loops in the letter *s* are a dead giveaway. Also look for sinistrogyric strokes.

* * *

Lying

Rare is the person who's never told a lie. But there's a wide gulf between someone who fibs, say, to be polite and someone who lies compuslively. Occasional fibbers don't give themselves away in their handwriting: While there are in fact more than two *dozen* individual signs that may indicate lying, one or two of these in a handwriting sample is no cause for suspicion. Isolated, individual signs do not necessarily signal lying. Rather, it's the accumulation of signs that will tip you off.

People with psychological problems are often intensely anxious, fearful, or depressed. As a result, they tend to make up stories and tell lies because it's easier than facing reality.

Compulsive liars are no different. If the liar is a close friend or business associate, the results can be devastating.

Say you spot half a dozen lying signals in your own script. Embarrassed, you work to change your writing—to wipe out the signs. You will succeed; however, without changing your behavior, six new signs will appear in your handwriting to replace the signs you've consciously rubbed out! Changing your handwriting is as hard as changing your fingerprints.

The following sample will prove instructive. See the section on Anxiety in Chapter 4 for more on the signs of lying.

Sale here and other shops in U.S. including City Lights, also under consideration to recite at the Polyphonix

Note the altered letters and strokes which make the writing difficult to read, as do the coils and overlapping strokes. Note the sinistrogyric slant. There are numerous capital letters in the middle of words, tapering words and strokes, and unfinished letters, as well as wide spacing in the middle of words.

Other common signs accumulate; embellished letters, reduced or irregular speed, meandering baseline, letters of different shapes and sizes, unnecessary dots, mainly after the signature. Very fast writing in thread letters or, very slow, tight writing can be signs as well.

The signature and the envelope address show a different handwriting when compared to the message.

REMEMBER: If a sample shows fewer than five or six of these signs, the writer is not necessarily dishonest. However, if you count more than six or seven specific factors, no matter which ones, watch out.

* * *

Moodiness

Various slants appear in the same samples along with a meandering baseline.

Physical Pain

Twisted letters. Irregular pressure.

* * *

Susceptibility

The susceptible person may easily fall prey to physical ailments. Psychologically, this person may also be easily influenced or hypersensitive.

Look for light pressure and unfinished letters and strokes.

* * *

Temper

Look for launching upward strokes.

* * *

Timidity

Missed not hearing from
wonder if it was as eventful
for me? Do write.

You will note tight, rather small letters, light pressure, unfinished letters and strokes, backward slant, and very large margins on all sides. Often, the signature is smaller than the writing in the sample and placed toward the left side of the paper, close to the writing above.

* * *

Unreliability

Caroline + I will raise our
glasses tonight + think of you
+ that wonderful piece of Paris
that is the Tumbleweed Hotel.

From the sample, would you peg this person as a liar? Certainly the signs are abundant: altered letters and threadlike connections make the script hard to read, as do the confused letters which flow into one another. The script appears slow and artificial. Note the meandering baseline; irregular pressure and size of letters; the hooks, coils, and embellished script; the backward slant. This person's signature likely is far different from his message.

* * *

Vengeful Person

Look for sinistrogyric, angular loops and strokes.

*   *   *

Weakness

Note the light, irregular pressure; thin, broken strokes; the unfinished letters. The meandering baseline also descends. Certain letters in the beginning or in the middle of a word float below the normal baseline of the zone to which they belong. Superfluous dots and twisted strokes are common.

2

IDENTIFYING PROBLEMS

With tools and terms at hand, you're ready now to apply your overall knowledge. The aim in this chapter is to develop your capacity to recognize, from the general aspect of the sample as a whole, whether or not the writer is basically healthy and well balanced. As you learn to "read" samples, you'll soon see that basic personality differences are easy to spot.

The general aspect of a sample depends on the various elements, especially pressure, baseline, slant, and stroke, *and* on their interaction. Multiple samples, gathered over time from the same writer, teach you to allow for the natural ebb and flow of the individual's disposition, the ups and downs of everyday life, and the mutual effects of the person on the situation and the situation on the person. Each sample becomes a snapshot that contributes to your overall portrait of the writer.

Just as there is a wide range of behaviors and emotions that you and I might agree are "normal" among any group of people, there is as well a wide range of handwriting that corresponds. When there is a problem, the script responds, as do behavior and emotion.

WHAT TO LOOK FOR

* * *

The General Aspect Is Fragmented

Pay attention to the margins, spacing, and signature. Watch for extremes, such as excessively large margins and word spacing or their opposites—small, tight, or absent margins or spacing. Is the signature similar to or very different from the message? Can you tell whether the speed is fast or slow? Speedy script is, in general, a more positive aspect than slow writing.

Pressure

Shaky writing (spasmodic pressure) usually means poor health and also signals specific diseases, as you'll see in the next chapter. People who have trouble, either in expressing or in controlling their emotions, may have shaky writing.

Your interpretation of extreme heavy pressure in the case of severely inhibited people will move away from "energy and general good health" and toward "suppressed emotions."

Very light pressure may signal a physically fragile person, a soaring intellect, nervousness or restlessness, or some combination of these traits.

Baseline

The path of the baseline gives you clues to disposition, overall energy level, and relative maturity. Ascending lines of script reveal heightened optimism, positive thinking, or perhaps flights of fancy. Descending lines indicate short- or long-term illness or depression.

A straight baseline is positive, and lines that meander have a wide range of specific interpretations. An extremely meandering baseline showing a very light pressure, for example, may indicate an acute problem (a temporary illness or an emotional upset) or long-term physical or emotional instability. The interplay of all elements is always important.

Slant

The accumulation or predominance of elements is important as well. Add to a meandering baseline and very light pressure the aspect of extremely variable slants within the same sentence or even the same word, and your interpretation will move toward the area of emotional instability, perhaps an anxious, nervous, or restless person prone to mood swings.

Some monotony in the script may reveal an artistic or creative person. A pronounced monotonous aspect may point to a psychological problem or even a disorder.

Shapes and Strokes

The Glossaries in Chapter 1 cover the individual shapes and strokes in detail. As with the other factors, shape alone carries very little meaning. To undertake a serious handwriting analysis, it's necessary to have more than one or two handwritten words in your sample. But a few lines of script or a short, spontaneous letter are sufficient to begin an interpretation. Remember to avoid photocopies, since they prevent you from knowing the writer's pressure.

Following is a short summary listing of some important shapes and strokes and their meanings. You will find this listing helpful as you begin to evaluate the samples in this chapter and the chapters ahead.

Altered strokes are an expression of anxiety or insecurity and may indicate moodiness, emotional instability, immaturity, or an irresponsible nature.

Arcades can denote arrogance, selfishness, or a deceitful or manipulative person.

Distorted or twisted script signals pain and physical illness, often a glandular disorder or a disease in a body organ.

Embellished script, which is one of the many individual signs of lying, might point to immaturity or a lack of formal education or a slow learning process.

Enlarged letters toward the end of a word imply gullibility.

High stems, loops, and/or i *dots* can be a sign of high, idealistic goals; active imagination; spirituality; intellectual frustration; or vanity.

Horizontal clubbed strokes betray an abrupt manner. The writer may have bisexual tendencies.

Inflated lower loops signal sexual ambivalence and/or sexual dreams or fantasies.

Inflated upper loops (round shape, upper zone) show a romantic and/or feminine nature.

Jumbled script—letters and lines flowing into one another—reveal mental confusion or possible substance abuse.

Launching upward strokes reveal that the writer has an active temper.

Long loops or strokes extending below the lower zone are signs of material or sexual frustration.

Overlapping or covered strokes: anxiety, depression, eating problems.

Pasty script: laziness, self-absorption, sexual fantasy or even acting out. Check the lower zone activity in the sample and form your opinion.

Sticklike script: selfishness; a brutal or ruthless nature.

Tapering strokes or words add a destructive aspect, such as a person whose sense of humor becomes caustic.

Vertical clubbed strokes are a sign of substance abuse and signal a separation of emotion from thought and behavior, called "deviated emotions," that often plague people who suffer a sudden, deep trauma or severe prolonged psychological disorder.

SAMPLES

Now you're ready for some detailed analyses. Remember that your main goal here is to gain an overall impression of the general state of the writer's physical or mental health. In this section, samples from healthy people are mixed in with samples from people who are not so fortunate.

   I've analyzed each sample in detail for you so that you can begin to acquire the skill which comes only from studying and comparing a great many handwriting samples. But don't lose sight of the whole: Your task here is to learn to identify the general elements that differentiate healthy from ill writers.

*   *   *

The Effects of Aging

Linda is a 26-year-old student.

Handwriting analysis:

- Large and round: femininity; need for affection and gratification.
- Convex initial strokes: sense of humor; optimism.
- Slightly meandering baseline: well-balanced character.
- Knotted loops: persistence; stubbornness.
- Connected script: deductive and analytical mind; sociable, attached to friends and family.
- Ringlets in the vowels: good business sense; seductive; manipulative.
- Coils: diplomacy; business acumen; attachment to money; selfishness.
- Strong, regular pressure: good health.

SHORT PORTRAIT OF LINDA: Linda is a normal, healthy, well-balanced young adult. Her business acumen is excellent. She is perseverant, diplomatic, and charming.

* * *

Hanna, 89, is in precarious physical health due to old age.

Handwriting analysis:

- Small: intelligent, creative, well educated.
- Light, irregular pressure: precarious health, various ailments.
- Fluctuating slant: mood swings.
- Speedy: quick, sharp mind, intelligent, vivacious.

- Very meandering baseline: mental instability; mood swings; depression.
- Thread letters: diplomacy; dissembling; fear.
- Altered strokes and letters: anxiety or anguish.
- Wide spacing: independence; inner loneliness.
- Tapering strokes: caustic humor; destructive tendencies.

SHORT PORTRAIT OF HANNA: She is very intelligent, her mind quick and sharp. Hanna is not senile. She still has a good sense of humor and a good memory. Hanna is very independent; she lives alone and is still able to take care of herself in spite of her advanced age.

Hanna is not especially compliant and may become impatient and nervous. Her moods are changeable. Extremely diplomatic, she is able to hide her feelings and lie when it is necessary. Generally speaking, considering her age, her handwriting is positive.

* * *

Anxiety

Jack, 29, is the eternal student. He works in various part-time jobs and plays chess.

Handwriting analysis:

- Angular: virile, ambitious, impatient, aggressive under stress.
- Fast: quick mind; vivacious, intelligent.
- Progressive slant: ambitious, dynamic, optimistic.
- Connected script: sociable, attached to friends and family.
- Tight spacing and overlapping, confused lines: lack of maturity; need for physical movement; mental confusion.
- Extremely large margin on the left-hand side: inhibited; anxious.
- Some hooks and tapering strokes: greedy; selfish; destructive tendencies.
- Strange, exaggerated, sticklike strokes: critical mind, neurosis.

JACK'S PORTRAIT: Jack's personality is contradictory. His mental health is precarious. Often his anxiety turns into anguish. This prevents him from working regularly, in spite of his intelligence and ambitions. He is not very happy. He needs a physical outlet in order to overcome his inner nervousness.

* * *

Stuart, 26, studies at an art school and hopes to become a serious painter.

Handwriting analysis:

- Round and connected: friendly and sociable; need for affection and gratification; ambivalence.
- Medium sized: well-balanced person.
- Easy to read: logical thinking; honesty.
- High *i* dots: imagination.
- Slightly meandering baseline: intelligence; well-balanced person.
- Regular, medium pressure: good health.
- Arcades: manipulative.
- Slightly progressive slant: optimistic; dynamic; ambitious.
- Open lower loops: fluctuating libido; ambivalence.
- Strong *t* crossings, slightly concave: strong willpower; good sense of humor.
- Normal spacing: well-balanced person.

BRIEF PORTRAIT: Unlike Jack in the preceding sample, Stuart is healthy, well balanced, and calm. He is intelligent, imaginative, honest, organized, and dynamic. He has a good sense of humor and should do well in his studies and later on in life. His handwriting and his libido are positive.

* * *

Emotional Instability

Paul, 47, works in public relations.

Handwriting analysis:

- Very meandering baseline: emotional instability.
- Very large: charming, vain, creative.
- Extremely large signature, very different from his script: diplomacy or deceit; the person is not trustworthy.
- Mainly round: charming and seductive; sexual ambivalence; need for affection.
- Fluctuating slant: instability; mood swings.
- Heavy, irregular *i* dots: neurotic tendencies; inner instability.
- Knotted loops: tenacity.
- Speedy script: vivacity; quick and sharp mind.
- Ringlets in several vowels: seductive; charming; sociable.
- Irregular spacing: instability; neurotic tendencies.
- Pronounced middle zone: need for affection and immediate gratification.
- Tapering strokes: destructive tendencies; inner aggression.

PAUL'S PORTRAIT: On the outside, Paul is very lively and sociable. In business, he knows how to charm and seduce people. His charm is rather feminine, and his sexuality is ambivalent. Paul is bisexual.

Public relations is well suited to Paul. He has a great need for affection and likes to be constantly surrounded and admired by others. His vanity is pronounced. With his artistic, theatrical talent, he could have become an actor. Paul is extremely diplomatic and capable of changing his attitudes and beliefs constantly. As a result he is unstable and fickle. When necessary, he can lie and hide his everchanging feelings. Therefore he is not very trustworthy.

Paul is extremely selfish, in spite of his apparent generosity and attachment to his friends. He suffers from mood swings and destructive tendencies: He's a "neurotic." Often he feels lonely and depressed. His libido is very ambivalent.

* * *

Edmond, 30, is the sales manager of a big import-export firm.

> After lunch I tried to find a public shower. This proved very difficult. I found one near the Pantheon

Handwriting analysis:

- Clear and easy to read: logical thinking; well-balanced, honest person.
- Progressive slant: dynamic; ambitious.
- Strong, regular pressure: good health.
- Slightly meandering baseline: intelligence; quick mind.
- Concave initial strokes: critical mind; sense of humor.
- Strong, regular *t* crossings: strong willpower.
- Knotted loops: tenacity.
- High *i* dots: imaginative; high, idealistic goals.
- Regular, normal spacing: Well-balanced, healthy person.
- Connected script: sociable; attached to friends and family.
- Medium to fast speed: intelligence; vivacity.
- Round and angular shapes: maturity; good health; well-balanced mind and libido.
- Closed lower loops of normal length: strong, virile libido.
- Ringlets in the vowels: business acumen; capacity to manipulate and seduce.

EDMOND'S PORTRAIT: Edmond's handwriting is very positive. He is emotionally stable—easy to work with and to live with.

His negative character traits are minimal. He is extremely healthy, physically and mentally. His mind is quick, and he is intelligent. He is well organized, dynamic, ambitious, and trustworthy. He has a good sense of humor.

Edmond's business sense is excellent. He is sociable and compliant. His willpower and his perseverance are good. In rare moments, Edmond can be selfish.

He is attached to his friends and quite generous, truthful, and honest. His libido is strong. (Remember, the libido includes zest for life, willpower, and sexuality.)

Edmond has manual and intellectual abilities as well as some latent artistic gifts.

* * *

Immaturity

Caroline, 24, is a college student working on an advanced education degree.

> Dear Sir or Madam, we are our
> year three B.Ed (hons) students
> in art at Chester College of the
> Education.
> Please could you inform us of a
> Vacancies you many have for th

Handwriting analysis:

- Large and round: feminine, sociable, and friendly; need for affection and immediate gratification; selfish.
- Regular, straight slant: lack of spontaneity; she thinks before she acts.

- Pronounced middle zone: selfish; indulgent; attachment to money.
- Slow, tight script: lack of maturity; economical
- Arcades: manipulative.
- Regular, strong pressure: good health.
- Straight baseline: well-balanced person; slightly stubborn.
- Coils: selfish; thrifty.
- Reduced spacing: juvenile and immature.

CAROLINE'S PORTRAIT: Caroline is a feminine and slightly childish young woman. She is extremely immature, has a great need for affection, and is very attached to other people. Her intelligence is in the low-average range, and her manual dexterity is good. Caroline is healthy and well balanced but not easy to live with.

*   *   *

Fergus, 32, studies archaeology. He is trying to finish his thesis.

Can't make it to
Paris this summer.
Best wishes to all
at. . inel Matteus,

Handwriting analysis:

- Slow: inhibited, lacks spontaneity; manipulative; dishonest; lacks maturity and intelligence.
- Backward slant: problems from the past which have not been overcome; egocentric; selfish, inhibited; lacks spontaneity, ambition, and dynamism; ability to concentrate, good memory.

- Extremely wide spacing: independent; need for freedom and autonomy; inner loneliness.
- Superfluous dots: the writer is distrustful; lying; slight emotional instability.
- Some hidden altered strokes: hypocrisy; anxiety; fear.
- Pronounced middle zone: selfish; need for affection, immediate gratification, and money.

BRIEF PORTRAIT OF FERGUS: At 32, his need for affection and reliance on others are exaggerated. His maturity and intellectual evolution are stunted. Fergus's attitude toward other people is childish and selfish. He is not ambitious and prefers to live in the past. (In this respect his studies are well chosen!) His reasoning is slow and cautious. Fergus does not trust anyone, and his inner fears make him untrustworthy as well. He is independent but very lonely and unhappy.

* * *

Pronounced Inhibitions

Gerald, 28, last worked in the research department of a large computer company.

> will accept it as nonetheless sincere. We
and look forward to you're coming home,
a breath — not to mention stabby drawer.
a special person you are, and never
than you deserve — apart from me, I can't
sing up! Although by the sound of
e — no, seriously, I've been thinking
said — and he sounds like quite a

Handwriting analysis:

- Angular: virile; inwardly nervous; vivacious, sharp mind; caustic and skeptical.
- Sinistrogyric: inhibited; dishonest; stubborn; neurotic tendencies.
- Upward launching strokes: temper tantrums; cruelty.
- Disconnected: independent; intuitive; the writer cannot be influenced.
- Angular arcades: arrogant; vain; selfish; a liar.
- Many tapering strokes: destructive and self-destructive tendencies.
- Tight spacing: great need for assistance from other people.
- Angular, regressive loops in the lower zone: vengeful.
- Altered, jumbled letters, difficult to read: Mental confusion.
- Pronounced middle zone: selfish; immature.
- Strong pressure: good physical health.
- Slow, artificial script: neurotic tendencies; stubborn.
- Overlapping strokes and loops: tenacity; fear; anxiety; anguish.

GERALD'S PORTRAIT: Like Fergus in the preceding sample, Gerald is painfully immature. He is intelligent but extremely inhibited. He is still wrestling with problems which occurred during his childhood. This struggle prevents him from maturing. He lacks spontaneity and faith in other people. His emotions and his behavior often are out of synch, and he is prone to mood swings and temper tantrums. His inferiority complex reveals itself in his excessive vanity.

Gerald is very independent and stubborn. His selfishness is almost childlike. Although he tries to think and reason before he acts, his mind often stays confused. At times Gerald shows aggression, violence, and vengefulness. He is very difficult to work with and to live with; he is not happy. His destructive and neurotic tendencies are strong.

Gerald stopped working one year ago. At present he is in psychoanalytic treatment.

* * *

Practice Exercise

Now glance briefly at the following handwriting sample. Is the writer inhibited, like Gerald, or anxious or immature? Are you beginning to see the overall contrasts in the script of basically well-adjusted people and those who are not?

Compared with Caroline, Fergus, and Gerald in the preceding samples, John's handwriting, which follows, is extremely positive.

* * *

John, 30, manages a small bookshop that he took over from his father. Business is good.

selection of English titles — sole extremely reasonable prices.

If you are interested in seeing what we have to offer, the we shall be pleased to see you Saturday at "The Scots Kirk,"

Handwriting analysis:

- Firm pressure: good physical health.
- Medium sized, easy to read: well-balanced personality; logical thinker.
- Shape, rather round: friendly, sociable character; emotional maturity, some ambivalence.

- Knotted loops: tenacity.
- Slightly meandering baseline: intelligence; quick mind; well-balanced person.
- Connected and disconnected script: sociable; attached to friends and parents; deductive and analytical mind.
- Initial strokes: critical mind.
- Pronounced middle zone: pragmatic; good business sense; hedonistic; need for affection.
- Progressive slant: dynamic; ambitious; optimistic; zest for life.

SHORT PORTRAIT: John's writing and his character are extremely positive. He's a good businessman—dynamic and hardworking, reliable, honest, and trustworthy. His physical and mental health are robust.

This is not to say that John's script reveals no negative aspects. For example, its pronounced middle zone reveals that John is a materialist who can give himself over to the pursuit of pleasure. But the positive aspects predominate: John is an emotionally mature man.

* * *

The Effects of Physical Illness

We begin with Laura, who, like John, is physically and mentally fit. *Laura is 27,* and works as a secretary and assistant manager in a firm that produces delicatessen and gourmet food products.

[handwriting sample] you and discussing Hand Writing Analysis when I was in Paris. I met you at op.

your card with the name of your book translated into English, unfortunately ?ard. I certainly would appreciate

Handwriting analysis:

- Slightly progressive slant: optimistic, spontaneous, dynamic.
- Regular and medium sized: well-balanced person; good mental health.
- Strong, regular pressure: good physical health.
- Easy to read: clear, logical thinking; respect for other people.
- Slightly meandering baseline: intelligent; well educated.
- Connected: sociable; attached to friends and family.
- High *i* dots: imaginative; idealistic goals.
- Strong, short *t* crossings; strong willpower.
- Overlapping strokes: discreet and diplomatic.
- Some arcades, coils, and hooks: excellent business acumen; greedy.
- Some slightly twisted loops in the lower zone: sexual ambivalence.
- Knotted loops in the lower part of the *s:* jealous or possessive.
- Regular, normal spacing: robust mental health; well-balanced person.
- Medium speed: a person who thinks before acting.
- Round shape: feminine; charming.

LAURA'S PORTRAIT: Generally speaking, Laura's handwriting is very positive. She is very healthy, mentally and physically—a hard worker with strong willpower. Her mind is critical, analytical, and deductive; her thinking is logical and focused.

Laura has an excellent visual memory and some artistic creativity. She is diplomatic and discreet yet trustworthy. She knows how to charm and manipulate others in business. She is organized, sociable, and adaptable. She is a leader. Along with her meticulous attention to her work, these traits will carry her far in her career.

In personal relationships, Laura craves affection. At times she can be selfish and possessive.

* * *

In contrast to Laura, *Ira, 72* years old, suffers from Parkinson's disease. The signs of physical illness are easy to see in his trembling handwriting.

Exposer franchement les avant
Il est important de souligner q.
grande tendanse à regarder les
et non pas les caractéristiques.
Il convient de dire, écrire et p

These samples show the difference between the script of healthy and ill people. We'll see more samples from people who are suffering from physical ailments in Chapter 3. The more samples you examine, the easier it will become to compare similar script features and to evaluate their meanings. A trembling handwriting like Ira's will make you think of a physically ill person at first sight.

Two other signs of sickness are light pressure and broken letters. Contrast Ira's script, above, with James's script, following.

* * *

Degrees of Psychological Disorder

James, 50 years old, is a published poet. His works are not well known. This sample is valuable both for the physical and psychological aspects it reveals in its writer.

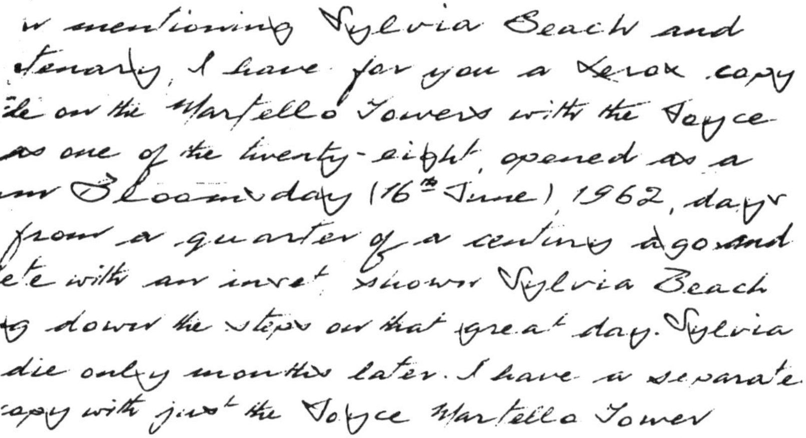
w mentioning Sylvia Beach and
tenary, I have for you a Xerox copy
le on the Martello Towers with the Joyce
as one of the twenty-eight, opened as a
um Bloomsday (16th June) 1962, days
from a quarter of a century ago and
ete with an insert shown Sylvia Beach
g down the steps on that great day. Sylvia
die only months later. I have a separate
copy with just the Joyce Martello Tower

James's handwriting is small, angular, and fast, revealing his intelligence, virility, quick mind, good education, and intellectual creativity. The light pressure and the irregular, broken strokes show that his physical health is precarious and that he suffers from cardiovascular problems (see Chapter 3).

The extremely progressive slant reveals his passion for his writing. However, there are many sinistrogyric, launching upward, and tapering strokes; James has strong destructive tendencies and often feels vengeful. His temper flares up unexpectedly. He is very impatient and intolerant. His behavior traits characterize the kind of person you and I probably would call "neurotic" (see Chapter 4).

* * *

Aurelia, 29, is an accountant. She is not working at the present time.

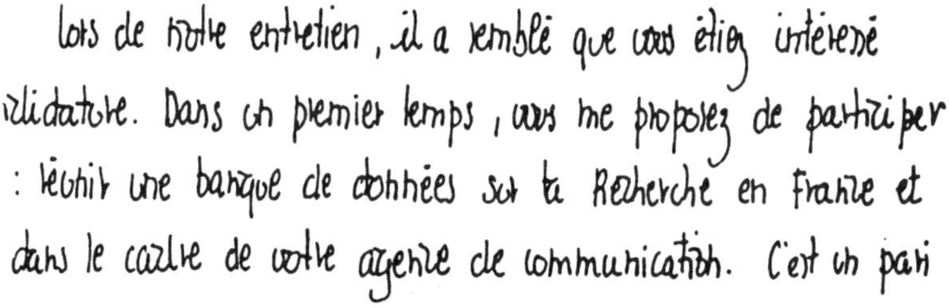
Lors de notre entretien, il a semblé que vous étiez intéressé
ilidature. Dans un premier temps, vous me proposez de participer
: réunir une banque de données sur la Recherche en France et
dans le cadre de votre agence de communication. C'est un pari

As you can see immediately, Aurelia's handwriting looks extremely monotonous and scholarly. There are unnecessary capital letters within the sentences. The pressure is very light and irregular. Many letters are unfinished. The script is artificial and very slow.

Aurelia suffers severe psychological distress, commonly called "psychosis," and has been in treatment for many years without much improvement. Her day-to-day functioning is impaired, and she has ceased to be a productive member of society.

* * *

Sandra, who is 29, hopes to become an actress but has not succeeded as yet.

Handwriting analysis:

- Straight ascending baseline: ambitious; dynamic; optimistic; strong willpower.
- Progressive slant: ambitious; zest for life; passion for work.
- Normal, regular spacing: well-balanced character.
- Connected writing: sociable; attached to friends.
- Round and angular shapes: intelligence; maturity.
- High *i* dots: imaginative; idealistic.
- Spasmodic pressure: deviated emotions; nervousness; emotional instability.
- Strange *t* crossings, tapering and pointing downward: destructive tendencies; aggression; violence; neurosis; anxiety; pessimism.
- Signature differs markedly from sample and points downward: pessimism; an untrustworthy person.

SANDRA'S PORTRAIT: Sandra is "high-strung." While on the one hand she is dynamic and ambitious and her mind is sharp (she is intelligent and well educated), on the other she is emotionally unstable and has a mean streak. Her destructive and self-destructive tendencies are strong.

Sandra's personality is riddled by contradictions. One moment she is caring, generous, and charming, then suddenly nasty, aggressive, even violent. Her deep-seated anxiety, combined with the depression provoked by her mood swings, hold Sandra back from achieving her idealistic and artistic goals. She is not completely trustworthy, lying mainly as a means to controlling her anxiety.

Her mental strength, sociability, and attachment to family and friends save her from plunging permanently into despair.

* * *

Daisy, 27 works for a big perfume distributor. She manages the promotions section of the marketing department and earns a good salary. Compare her handwriting with the preceding samples from James, Aurelia, and Sandra.

Handwriting analysis:

- Easy to read: clear, well-balanced mind.
- Medium sized: intelligent; optimistic.
- Slant slightly progressive: dynamic; ambitious; optimistic; spontaneous.
- Fairly fast: quick mind; intelligent.
- Round with ringlets in the vowels: feminine, charming; seductive.
- Well-balanced zones: logical thinking; well-balanced personality.
- Strong, regular pressure: good health.
- Fluctuating *t* crossings: fluctuating willpower.
- Knotted loops: perseverance.
- Some arcades: capacity to manipulate others.
- Slightly meandering baseline: intelligence; good mental balance.
- High *i* dots: imagination; high goals; ambition.
- Initial, straight strokes at the beginning of each word: critical mind.

- Connected script: deductive and analytical thinking; sociability; attachment to friends.

PORTRAIT OF DAISY: She is both healthy and emotionally well balanced. Her intelligence and maturity are above the average. Daisy is ambitious, dynamic, and has an excellent business sense: She is capable of selling anything—even a nonexistent product! It's not surprising that her career is progressing so well.

Daisy is logical, realistic, and responsible. She is imaginative and optimistic. She loves her work. Her engaging personality makes her fun to be with and easy to live with. She's a happy person.

Periodically, Daisy gets tired and lazes the day away, but her persistence compensates for these moments of weariness.

*   *   *

Helen, 53, formerly a journalist, now lives in a residential treatment facility. These few lines of writing reveal the traits that contributed to Helen's current condition.

Handwriting analysis:

- Extremely meandering baseline: mental instability; strong mood swings.
- Irregular pressure and size: deviated emotions, emotional instability; drug or alcohol abuse.
- Broken strokes: high blood pressure.

- Tapering strokes and words: destructive tendencies; aggression.
- Speedy: vivacious; quick thinking; intelligent.
- Superfluous capital letters: neurotic tendencies.
- Progressive slant: dynamic; ambitious.
- Altered letters: dishonest; hypocritical; psychotic tendencies.
- Connected script: sociable; attached to friends.
- Angular shapes: masculine; dynamic; cruel.
- Large, irregular spacing: independent; need for freedom; lonely.

HELEN'S PORTRAIT: Even if you don't read French, you can read Helen's personality in this sample. Physically she is frail, suffering from high blood pressure. Emotionally, she is in treatment for manic-depressive disorder. Left to her own devices, she drinks heavily, to the point that she can be considered an alcoholic.

Helen's precarious mental state wrecked her career as a journalist. Even with medication, she can become extremely depressed or go out of control, becoming agitated, boisterous, or bursting into tears without reason. Her mental condition has exacerbated her physical woes. She requires constant medical attention.

Note the abundant signs of lying in her script. Her anxiety, insecurity, and instability feed her destructive and self-destructive tendencies.

* * *

A Special Case

As a rule, at this early stage in your study of graphology I recommend against trying to tackle the analysis of a renowned person's handwriting. A person of genius usually has an extravagant hand, which cannot be used to reinforce your knowledge of the characteristics most of us share. Many artists suffer from extremely strong, or even deviated, emotions: Their "craziness" is released when they create. Robbed of their creativity, many would become mentally disordered.

That said, consider the script of the famous writer, Ernest Hemingway, in the following sample. Hemingway committed suicide in 1961, tragically ending a life of unreined passions, from covering wars and insurrections to hunting big game, from alcoholism to womanizing.

Hemingway had a vigorous, egocentric personality, but his libido was unsatisfying and sexually ambivalent. Note the many ink-filled letters and the large, often open, lower loops. His writing is connected, rather tight, and slightly regressive, which reveals his need for affection and his selfishness. The strong pressure of the sample points up Hemingway's robust health, the high *i* dots his imagination.

Finally, note the signature, complete with paraph, which crosses out the name, thus signaling a self-destructive nature. The positive aspect of his signature matching his script in the message is offset by its negative, descending baseline.

* * *

The Effects of Stress

Some folks work best under pressure; others will go to any length to avoid stress. Obviously, we experience stress subjectively, but the objective fact is that too much stress can debilitate both body and spirit. Ursula, in the first sample, is thriving, while Marilyn, the second sample, is folding under the stress of her life.

* * *

Ursula, 35, is an assistant editor in a publishing house.

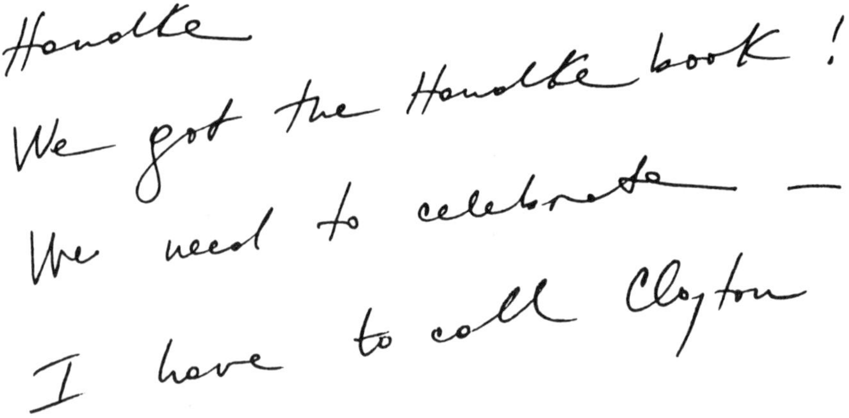

Handwritten note:

Handle

We got the Handle book !

We need to celebrate —

I have to call Clayton

Handwriting analysis:

- Very speedy: intelligent; quick, sharp mind; good education.
- Rather small: intelligent; intellectual creativity.
- High upper stems: high, idealistic goals; intellectual frustration.
- Progressive slant: dynamic; strong willpower; ambitious; optimistic.
- Wide spacing: independent; intellectual and emotional isolation.
- Easy to read: clear, logical thinking; respect for others.

- Connected script: sociable; adaptable.
- Strong *t* crossings: willpower; hard working.
- Tapering strokes: destructive tendencies; caustic sense of humor; critical mind.
- Some coils: business acumen.
- Clubbed end strokes: inner impatience; ability to push friends away.
- Irregular, medium pressure: slight, latent, physical health problems.

SHORT PORTRAIT: Ursula's sharp mind and quick, imaginative intellect enable her to work independently and creatively. She is trustworthy, and her personality is well balanced. Her business sense is excellent. Ursula clearly has chosen a position well suited to her abilities.

* * *

Marilyn, 38, is a sales manager in a fast-paced, high-pressure industry.

Handwriting analysis:

- Speedy: intelligent; quick, sharp mind; good education.
- Medium sized with high stems in the upper zone: intellectual frustration.

- Round and angular: intelligent; logical.
- Knotted loops: tenacity; persistence.
- Ringlets: charm; seductiveness.
- Overlapping strokes: diplomacy; ability to dissemble and lie; tenacity.
- Altered letters and strokes: fear; lying; anxiety; anguish.
- Progressive slant: dynamic; ambitious; optimistic; spontaneous.
- Tapering end strokes: destructive and self-destructive tendencies.
- Meandering and slightly plunging baseline: instability; depression.
- Light, irregular pressure: deviated emotions; anxiety; cardiovascular problems.
- Some thin, almost broken strokes: cardiovascular weakness.
- Long, closed loops in the lower zone: materialistic and sexual frustration.
- Connected writing: sociable; attached to friends and family.

PORTRAIT OF MARILYN: This sample illustrates a person in precarious physical and mental health. Certainly her fast-track career is contributing to the frustration evident in her handwriting. Work pressures fuel her emotional instability and place physical stress on her cardiovascular system, which by nature appears weak. Marilyn is impatient and nervous. Her inner anxiety places further stress on her heart. She should have her blood pressure checked.

I suspect that Marilyn is not easy to live with, at work or at home. She is uncompromising and hides her feelings. Her personality appears extremely contradictory, and her emotions are deviated (they do not correspond to her conscious thoughts and intentions).

3

PHYSICAL ILLNESS

By analyzing the samples in this chapter you will hone your developing ability to differentiate healthy from ill writers and to detect signs of physical discomfort or illness. It is relatively easy to recognize signs of physical illness in writing samples. Of course, handwriting analysis cannot diagnose specific illnesses as a doctor can, but you will be surprised at just how much about a person's health you can glean from studying handwriting samples.

A number of physical ailments can be detected with precision. Cardiovascular illness, for example, is evident from its early stages. It makes sense: the heart pumps blood through the body, right down to the fingertips. An irregular or weak heartbeat has immediate repercussions on the script. The same holds true for high or low blood pressure, excessive cholesterol, and the potential for heart attack, as you'll soon discover.

You encountered one sample from a victim of Parkinson's disease in Chapter 2, and more samples are coming up. In this chapter, you will learn the interrelated signs for disorders such as ulcers, asthma, rheumatism, Alzheimer's disease, and even thyroid disorders.

Although recognizing the graphic signs of physical illness

is easy, discovering the precise nature of the illness is a task for the medical professional, who in examining the patient can ask how it feels and where it hurts. For you as an amateur graphologist, the ability to recognize signs of physical ailments might make a difference in whom you hire or in your attitude toward a loved one. You might be able to suggest consultation with a medical professional for someone you can see is suffering, before even they are aware of any disorder.

Once again, the brief catalog of physical ailments that follows is organized alphabetically. And since the physical and the psychological aspects of health intertwine, you will note as well some references to Chapter 4, where conditions that affect our mental well-being are cataloged.

*   *   *

Alcoholism (See Substance Abuse.)

ALZHEIMER'S DISEASE

This dreaded brain disease usually affects older people—10 percent of those 75 and older and 20 percent of those 85 and older. United States Census Bureau estimates of the total number of Alzheimer's victims at between 2 and 4 million make it the fourth leading cause of death among Americans. Only heart disease, cancer, and strokes kill more each year. Though untreatable at present, continuing advances in the search for the genetic and biochemical triggers of Alzheimer's promise hope for its treatment and eventual cure.

As the disease runs its course over as few as 3 and as many as 20 years, the gradual physical deterioration of the brain manifests itself in a gradual loss of memory and reasoning. In the beginning there are moments of relief; everything seems normal. But as Alzheimer's progresses, the patient may lose all sense of reality—failing even to recognize loved ones. As mental functions deteriorate, handwriting deteriorates as well, and the script becomes:

- Uneven and difficult to read, with unfinished strokes.
- Irregular (the hand trembles), with altered letters and over-lapping strokes.
- Slow, usually with light pressure and meandering or down-ward-plunging baseline.

Samples follow.

* * *

Senility

A small proportion of the aged may suffer progressive brain damage due perhaps to a series of small strokes, a tumor on the brain, or alcoholism. All cause senility. Healthy living and intellectual exercise are the best ways to stave off this condition. Use it or lose it is good advice. Signs of senility in the handwriting are similar to those of Alzheimer's disease, as the following samples reveal.

* * *

Arthritis (See Joint and Bone Diseases.)

ASTHMA

Asthma may be an allergic reaction, to pollen and spores, to microorganisms in sand or dust, to a pet's fur, to polluted air. The disease is on the increase worldwide. In the United States, there are 10 million asthmatics. That's 4 in every 100 people, up from 3 in 100 in 1979.

In the samples that follow, note the many superfluous dots—in the middle of a stroke and between letters, words, and lines. The spacing is irregular, and the pressure is spasmodic. Overlapping or altered strokes are common.

Psychological factors may contribute to asthma, but this is unproved.

* * *

Blood Pressure (See Cardiovascular Deficiencies.)

CANCER

This second leading cause of death among Americans accounts for more than one-fifth of the total each year. The body of a cancer victim becomes weak. The person is always tired and sleeps more and more. There may be a sudden weight loss and emotional changes.

Like the number-one killer, heart disease, cancer may be strongly influenced by a person's temperament and habits, among them eating and drinking patterns, reactions to stress, and smoking.

Handwriting undergoes brutal changes, which are easiest to spot if you have access to samples of the script written when the person was healthy. In general you will note that the following aspects are intensified in the script of people suffering from cancer:

- Weak, even limp, pressure.
- Round shapes and garlands.
- Difficult-to-read script: twisted strokes and letters in all zones; broken strokes; altered letters.
- Descending baseline; end strokes and letters plunging below the baseline.
- Heavy *i* dots.

Samples follow.

23·12·86

Dear George,

have arrived we
safely in the algarve.

Phantasie, er ist sehr
heu. Trotz seiner Offenhei
zichkeit verstedet sich eine
e Arcogany, denn er wre,
21 wed if. Er ist sehr eup
Er verstedet seine Gefühle.

* * *

CARDIOVASCULAR DEFICIENCIES

Heart disease and stroke combine to cause more than 40 percent of deaths annually in the United States. Improper diet, reactions to stress, and smoking are prime promoters of high cholesterol levels and high blood pressure, which contribute to cardiovascular deficiency.

Following are samples from people who have suffered heart attacks. Note the extremely light, spasmodic pressure combined with broken and altered strokes. The script is difficult to read.

Dear Claude,
This morning I decided
walk to my meeting he
was raining. — fortunately
stopped by the time han
came around,

Barbara,

I'm enjoying this weekend

* * *

Low Blood Pressure

A person whose blood pressure is low has less stamina than someone at the healthy norm. But while these people tend to start slower and to feel the cold or heat more, they tend as well to last longer—to be persistent at tasks and resistant to many diseases. The following samples were written by people with very low blood pressure, which is a difficult aspect to isolate in the script. Note the light pressure, occasional ink-filled vowels, few *t* crossings. Some letters are unfinished. Finally, compare the general aspect of these samples from relatively healthy writers with those of the heart attack victims above.

* * *

To summarize, these are the aspects of handwriting which may indicate cardiovascular deficiency:

- Extremely light, irregular pressure; trembling and shaking script.
- Very meandering baseline combined with broken strokes.
- Baseline plunging downward; letters plunging suddenly downward, below the baseline.
- Superfluous dots inside the strokes, letters, words, or lines.
- The letter *o* in a heart shape.
- Vowels and loops filled with ink.
- Altered shapes and letters.

Several of these factors relate to illness as a general aspect of the writer. The most specific signal is the heart-shaped *o*, which often appears in the script of people who know they have heart disease. If the writer is in doubt about your interpretation of cardiovascular deficiency, urge him or her to have a blood pressure or cholesterol checkup.

* * *

High Blood Pressure

The specific sign is precise and easy to detect: Thin or broken strokes appear suddenly in stems and loops, as shown here.

⌣ heard a 1000 blended notes,
while in a grove I sat reclined.
In that sweet mood when pleas-
ant thoughts,
Bring sad thoughts to the mind.

from Early Spring

Chère Claude

La soirée est très sympathique,
les gens sont souriants.
C'est la nuit de la pleine nuit
les gremlins vont bientôt sortir.

* * *

Excessive Cholesterol Level

Too much cholesterol in the blood raises blood pressure and puts a strain on the heart. In the samples that follow, can you find at least one heart-shaped *o*? You will see many general signs of physical stress or illness, too, in the script of these adults with elevated cholesterol levels.

and so your spirits
are alive in the store.
Sending you love
and our thoughts —
Karen

square Emmanuel chálice
0 17 Paris

this is not too late a date or

you suggest possible places to st

* * *

Psychological Factors

Certain forms of high blood pressure result from prolonged stress (recall Marilyn, the last sample in Chapter 2). People with intense, reactive temperaments—whether directed outward or within—face the risk of constricted arterial walls and excess salt and water retention, leading to elevated blood pressure and the prospect of heart problems. Note in the following samples the apparent spasmodic pressure, broken strokes, and plunging baselines. Altered letters and overlapping strokes make the script difficult to read.

Dear Martin,

I'm in Paris

The.

* * *

Cholesterol (See Cardiovascular Deficiencies.)

Drug Abuse (See Substance Abuse.)

GLANDULAR DISORDERS

The glands that comprise the human endocrine system regulate and influence metabolism and growth, mood, and sexual behavior. The system works by secreting hormones manufactured in the glands into the bloodstream. Atop the kidneys, the adrenal glands secrete adrenaline in times of stress. The ovaries and testes secrete sex hormones. Regulated by the brain, the pituitary gland releases hormones that influence the activity of the other glands.

* * *

Pituitary Disorder

At puberty the surge of hormonal activity throughout the body makes mild fluctuations in pituitary secretions common, for beyond its role as the "master gland," the pituitary also secretes the hormone that regulates body growth. Synthetic growth hormone, produced through genetic engineering, now is available to treat people who lack sufficient levels in their system to allow normal growth.

In the sample, note these signs of pituitary disorder:

- Twisted strokes in the middle zone (use your magnifying glass).
- Strokes that appear suddenly broken off.
- Heavy *i* dots and punctuation marks.

*experience ι find "angst ι
because I've read widely
already intellectually how
fully experienced everythin(
me because it isn't em
base my opinions an z"
a result of my study*

* * *

Thyroid Disorder

Situated near the neck, the thyroid also contributes to body growth and to the growth and condition of our hair, skin, and nails. An overactive thyroid can affect mood as well as appearance.

Handwriting analysis reveals twisted and clubbed strokes as well as spasmodic pressure, as in this sample:

-pendant les quelles je dees comme une

Il me semble que depuis 6 mois m<

en plus clinble

Vale donc en quelques mots

* * *

JOINT AND BONE DISEASES

Bone disease may be organic or result from physical injury. Arthritis, or inflammation of the joints, affects millions. Rheumatism, which affects muscles as well as joints, is less common but more severe. In children and young adults who have contracted rheumatic fever, the inflammation and pain also affect the heart muscle. The swelling and pain arthritis and rheumatism cause may discourage their victims from writing.

The most obvious graphic signal of joint or bone problems is a twisted stroke in the middle and lower zones. Use your magnifying glass to examine the following samples.

I visit you with

journey to England,

of these remaining books.

, them but should be agree-

tional discounts and also

?ew books or sets from y<

Please let me know,

Sq Emmanuel Chabrier
75017 .

Jechnologie et puis j'ai
des dependiz au
Telephone.

-tion a déjà été l'objet de
-s antérieures. Les professeurs de
y ont ennoncé des propositions

LIVER DISEASE

The liver once was thought to be a factor in determining a person's temperament. Considering its influence on digestion and excretion and on the manufacture of blood sugar from the food we eat, the liver undoubtedly does contribute to our feelings of well-being.

Liver problems may manifest themselves in headaches, fever, heartburn, or even vomiting. Bad breath is another common symptom. Of course, these symptoms apply to many diseases.

Likewise, the characteristic handwriting features of liver

disease are common to other ailments. The following aspects
will appear in the script:

- Light, irregular pressure.
- Thread letters and connections.
- Pasty script with altered and/or ink-filled letters.
- Strokes become thicker toward the baseline (use your mag-
  nifying glass to see this).

Here are samples:

Cirrhosis of the Liver

Often a disease of alcoholics, cirrhosis (fibrosis of the liver) can prove fatal. A characteristic trembling appears mainly in vertical handwriting strokes:

For Example,

* * *

PARKINSON'S DISEASE

You encountered the handwriting of Ira, who suffers Parkinson's, in the Chapter 2 section, The Effects of Physical Illness. Like Alzheimer's, senility, heart disease, and alcoholism, a trembling stroke characterizes Parkinson's and other diseases. Note here the combination of trembling stroke and light pressure. You may want to turn back to Ira's sample in Chapter 2 and compare the two samples.

Dear Uncle, I am writing this at your request as a specimen my handwriting, - in order that may establish my character. I un that this is not much to work on the slips movement is causing me problems.

* * *

Rheumatism (See Joint and Bone Disease.)

Schizophrenia (See Chapter 4.)

Senility (See Alzheimer's Disease.)

Stress (See Cardiovascular Deficiencies and Ulcers; see also Chapter 2.)

SUBSTANCE ABUSE

Dependence on alcohol and drugs has psychological as well as physical roots. (See the section, A Note on Substance Abuse, in Chapter 4.) Addiction takes place over a period of time, and so it is most helpful to have a series of samples that predates the person's first drug use and progresses through the ages and stages of dependence.

It is not always possible to discern the handwriting of an alcoholic from that of a heavy drug user. Regardless of the nature of the dependence, as abuse grows into addiction, you will note the graphic signals of disease:

• The whole sample has a fragmented appearance.
• Spacing between letters and words is irregular.
• Pressure is light or irregular.
• Baseline meanders or plunges or both.
• The slant fluctuates.
• Shapes and strokes are altered, twisted, or broken.

*   *   *

Addiction to Heroin

To give you a feel for the general handwriting aspect of drug dependent people, following are four samples from heroin addicts of varying ages. You can see the physical and mental deterioration at a glance. In each sample, the confusion of the script, the altered letters, the meandering baseline, and the fluctuating slant are pronounced.

Girl of 19

* * *

Man of 34

* * *

Woman of 40

...h you still want t...

...when you ge I bu...

...ite me. if you ge a...

...e love...

*   *   *

Man of 27

With the name wr... ___ an
prove faithful & bright. i
gave off in many ___ a
with a feel 4 breezes.
I write "help, help me out of the

*   *   *

Alcoholism

In differentiating the script of alcoholics, following, from that of drug users in the preceding samples, note that in general alcohol abusers write fast, with a progressive slant. Usually, pressure is irregular, and the clubbed strokes frequently appear. At advanced stages, the handwriting looks strange or confused.

Man of 35

* * *

ANALYSIS: This man, who has studied literature and music, is in treatment. Did you find the sample difficult to read? The letters are of many shapes and sizes. The spacing is sometimes wide and at other times absent. The baseline meanders and plunges downward. The pressure is slightly irregular. And note the heavy *i* dots. As alcoholics sometimes slur their spoken words, note here the slurred word "remer" for "remember."

* * *

Man of 22

ANALYSIS: Rather than pursuing his career goals, this young man is in an alcohol rehabilitation program. His strong self-destructive tendencies and resulting depression combine to encourage drinking binges during which he downs whiskey until he loses consciousness.

Take another look at the handwriting sample. The numerous coils and ringlets reveal self-centeredness, yet the variety of letters, the altered and overlapping strokes point to confusion, immaturity, and anguish. Some letters fall below the meandering baseline, reinforcing the notion of emotional instability and depression. The tapering end strokes indicate self-destruction.

* * *

Woman of 46

The final example in this section is a series of samples written by a long-time drinker. Thanks to a sizeable inheritance, she has no money worries—and nothing to fill her time. Due to multiple traffic incidents while under the influence, she no longer enjoys the privilege of driving.

She has a long-term history of mental instability. Her emotions are volatile. She is restless and does not sleep much. Hers is an unhappy story and a wasted life.

In the samples that follow, note the many handwriting styles this woman uses, as well as the common aspect of deterioration that permeates the samples.

What do you think of
my new enterprise?
it's almost finished
how; why don't you
visit? Love,

Many thanks — long
overdue — for your
very kind hospitality

"hospitat

I enjoyed

much — You

Analysis: Like her mind, her handwriting is confused. Words and letters are entangled and difficult to read. The size is large—even oversized—and the shape round: she is feminine, charming, and affectionate—to the point of cloying. Here, the tapering, sometimes angular strokes within the round aspect reinforce the notion of confusion and destructive tendencies.

The irregular pressure is a clue to her alcoholism, as are the sticklike strokes and tapering word endings. These signs, along with the great variety of handwriting styles, reflect not only her instability and self-destructive tendencies but also her potential for inflicting harm on others. Regardless of the script style she uses, the handwriting is confused, with altered letters, backward slant, heavy i dots, meandering baseline.

* * *

Drug Dependence

In contrast to the script of alcohol dependent people, drug users typically write slowly. The aspect may be monotonous. But again, it's not always possible to identify specific drugs from one another or from alcohol. Take a look back at the samples under Addiction to Heroin, earlier in this section. To complicate matters, many drug abusers also abuse alcohol.

In fact, it's not always easy to detect drug use via handwriting analysis. Among the addicted, some are young teenagers; some middle-aged professionals. Some are poor and undereducated; some enjoy wealth and privilege. Many are in good physical health, though their psychological selves are hurting. Handwriting may be slow, even regressive; childlike; and monotonous, with heavy pressure. In advanced stages, the script may become confused, fast, and difficult to read, that is, more like the alcohol abuser.

Here are two more samples. The first is the writing of a

man in the early stages of drug abuse; the other is the script of an addict. Note from the regular, firm pressure that both still enjoy good physical health. The fluctuating slants and baselines and the altered letters reveal their more precarious mental conditions. Note especially the clubbed strokes and heavy *i* dots in Zita's sample.

Samuel is 23

e   here,   you're   welcome

over.   You   know   my

I   I'm   on   the   ESC   (stairway)   C,
(don't count the ground floor
- but there are numbers to help you!),   door

ht.   Ring   the   doorbell   - it

be   home   tonite   but   don't

10pm   because   there   is   a   code

and   you'll   have   trouble

ee   you   soon.

*   *   *

Zita is 31

and pevrier !

ue is ~~x~~ mai

pink like a

you enjoy the

s of this rubbi-

s Sincerely

* * *

ULCERS

Psychological states such as prolonged anxiety can affect the digestive tract by stimulating excess digestive fluids, which eat away parts of the lining of the stomach or small intestine. The result is an ulcer.

Individual reactions to prolonged stress may trigger the same bodily response, just as an intense, reactive personality can affect cardiovascular health. During adolescence, physical and mental "growing pains" may temporarily create a similar effect, which disappears in basically healthy young adults.

Ulcers are painful, and the handwriting shows it. Some letters plunge below the descending baseline. Twisted, altered, and covered strokes abound. If in the healthy state a person's script shows a progressive slant, it suddenly will shift to a straight or even a backward slant. Gradually the writing speed will slow. Curiously, the pressure generally will be regular and strong.

Note that often you will see twisted, angular, back-slanting strokes in the lower-zone loops. Since these strokes are typical of vengeful traits in the personality, the old adage that hate "eats away" at people rings of truth.

Now analyze the following samples written by three people with ulcers.

Having seen some
magnificent scenery in
New South Wales, we are
now having a 'rest' on this
coast in Queensland & visiting
an Island to see some coral

Votre émission de mardi
avec plusieurs messieurs
pas fait rire, mais plutot
. Ce monsieur Albert Lecoq
ainsi sa haine des femmes
e vision monstrueuse de
rdu. La haine et l'amour
mmandent pas. Il n'est rien

Yes, the cars are a bit small — bu

think? Well, it makes

this with my love,

again before very long.

Yuletide Greetings

Yours

4

PSYCHOLOGICAL
WELL-BEING

Psychological as well as physical states are evident in the handwriting or any graphic expression. Art therapists work with children and adults, using painting and drawing to assess inner feelings and to help people who are troubled to identify and work through their mental problems. Psychologists have even studied the paintings of schizophrenia victims, seeking to interpret their mental states. Graphology, from handwriting analysis to graphic exercise and therapy, is a therapeutic tool that is available to everyone.

We gauge our own well-being by how happy, healthy, or prosperous we feel. Yet there is nothing as difficult to define as "normal" behavior. Psychologists have defined and cataloged types of maladaptive, or "disordered," behaviors—ways of thinking and acting that strike the observer as atypical or disturbing or unjustifiable. You don't have to think hard to come up with at least one person you know—or know of—whose behavior fits the bill. Perhaps it's the celebrity who can't seem to get enough attention and love, or the tycoon who's always amassing more money or real estate or political power. Perhaps it's the notorious criminal, who steals or even kills without remorse. Perhaps it's the neighborhood "crazy," who never leaves the house. Or the one who rants ceaselessly on a city street.

WHAT TO LOOK FOR

In order to increase your skill, you will proceed by analogy through the samples in this chapter, comparing them with the samples in preceding chapters and with samples you've collected on your own. It's a tricky business: In the beginning, you will need to work hard to distinguish specific characteristics. Yet the experience you've gained in your study to date will help you as you analyze what follows. Similar samples of script reveal common traits. Even if no two handwriting samples are exactly the same, even if they are written in a language foreign to you, you still will gain insight into the writer's unique or overriding personality traits. The relevant similarities yield useful information and will help you to develop your observational skills, your intuition, and your recall.

At the broadest level, people with pronounced psychological problems experience difficulty in communicating with others and in controlling their feelings, thoughts, and behavior. Consciously or unconsciously, people who suffer mental disorders usually try to mask their conditions. You might talk with them for hours without a hint as to their plight. Yet a glance at their handwriting sample will reveal to you, for example, an abundance of individual signs of lying, which will increase in the handwriting regardless of the person's success in obscuring an inner psychological problem.

As always, the easiest way to diagnose the current state of a writer is to have access to a range of samples written at different times. If you know the characteristic patterns of a healthy, well-adjusted person's script, you will see at a glance when that person is suffering, psychologically or physically.

As a general guide, the following characteristics mark the handwriting of a person with psychological problems.

* * *

Confused Script

Walter, 44

He has spent many years in a home for mentally disabled people. At the present time his family takes care of him at home. Walter can only scribble strange, impossible-to-read words on paper. When he talks, his sentences do not make much sense. He still undergoes treatment on an out-patient basis. We do not have to analyze his script or his character in depth. His letters are altered, confused, and reveal a variety of shapes, sizes, and slants. The *i* dots are strange and heavy. Walter's mind is completely confused.

* * *

Heddy, 56

> L they like to employ is to my mind too
> vg at best. I encountered many
> polite and with a touch of understatena
> age free-thinking, far-ranging
> educational systems are designed to
> he social structuring. It's just a little
> t of technological and communication
> iomorality norms or religious
> being one who could not, and would
> not learning under the auspices of
> religious organisation. I suffered
> in't go to school, and when I did

Heddy is married and the mother of two. She has never worked outside the home. Her handwriting is slow, juxtaposed, and entangled. The lower loops reveal regressive, inflated, and tapering strokes. All in all, a very confused aspect.

Heddy is psychotic. She suffers from problems in her past which she cannot overcome and often feels frustrated and vindictive. Her destructive tendencies are strong. Regular exercise and other physical outlets would help her to improve her general outlook and energy level.

Note that the script in this sample is slightly monotonous and looks childlike. The many arcades, especially in the *m*'s,

reveal that Heddy is rather manipulative. She is very feminine but also childish.

*   *   *

Extremes of Pressure/Irregular Pressure

Bruno, 29

Bruno killed a policeman during an attempted bank robbery. He was sentenced to prison for twenty years. Beyond
the confused aspect of his script (altered letters, meandering
baseline, fluctuating slant, and unfinished strokes), note the
extremely light pressure in contrast to the rather heavy punctuation and *i* dots.

Bruno is emotionally unstable. His emotions are deviated. This is evident in the combination of unfinished strokes (which indicate insecurity and timidity) alongside strokes that are tapering, often sinistrogyric, and extremely angular (indicating violence and aggression). Some letters show coils, which I interpret in this case as greed, selfishness, and sexual acting out.

Without treatment, Bruno will likely remain unhappy and aggressive even when he regains his freedom.

* * *

Sandra, 55

The heavy pressure of this script reveals great inner violence, as do the sinistrogyric strokes and strong *t* crossings. Note in addition the confused aspect of Sandra's handwriting: entangled letters, lines, and lower loops; overlapping strokes and loops. (The latter indicate as well Sandra's egocentricity. She is persistent to the point of stubbornness.)

Sandra is institutionalized and involved in long-term psychoanalysis. Her mental condition is revealed not only by the extreme pressure of her script but also by its slow speed, the letters that plunge below the baseline, and by occasional capital letters in the middle of words.

Evident as well are Sandra's great need for affection (round shapes) and extreme attachment to others (entangled letters and lines). Her relative intelligence level is low (evident in the slow, heavy script).

* * *

Jurgen, 23

The pressure of his handwriting is very irregular. The script has a childlike, monotonous aspect. Note the descending baseline as well. Jurgen is under medical supervision (psychoanalysis and drug therapy) as a result of an attempt on his brother's life.

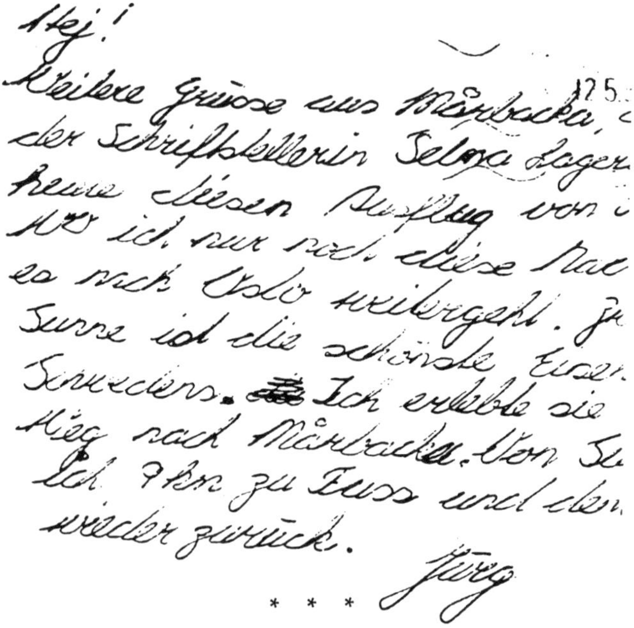

[handwritten sample in German, signed "Jürg"]

* * *

Meandering or Descending Baseline

Anthony, 73

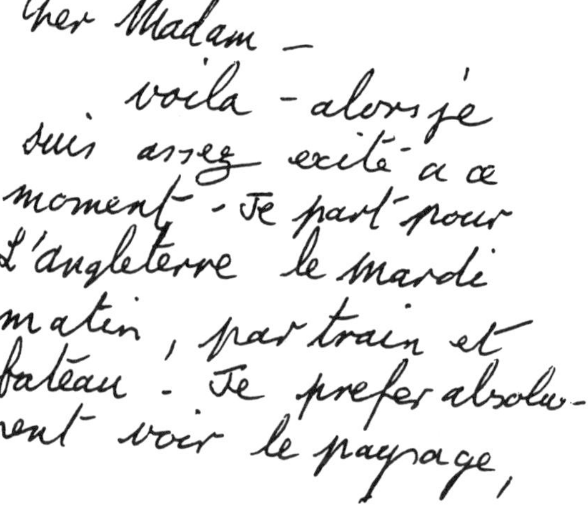

[handwritten sample in French:]

Cher Madam —
voila — alors je
suis assez exité a ce
moment - Je part pour
L'angleterre le mardi
matin, par train et
bateau - Je prefer absolu-
ment voir le paysage,

Anthony is retired and in good physical health, evident in the pressure. He always planned to become an artist but never realized his potential. He has spent many years in treatment for his psychological woes.

Here the baseline is extremely meandering, often a sign of emotional instability and mental disorder. Occasional altered letters and heavy *i* dots and punctuation reinforce this interpretation. The numerous tapering strokes point to an active temper, moodiness, and destructive aspects of Anthony's personality. Some letters and even entire lines plunge downward, revealing Anthony's depression.

* * *

Bill, 44

Although his intelligence is above average, Bill's chronic depression, emotional instability, and anxiety frustrate all his efforts. He has undergone psychoanalysis for the past ten years, yet he still finds it impossible to interact with other people. When he opened his own import-export company, he went bankrupt within one year. This is due in large part to turnover: He was unable to keep any employee for more than a couple of weeks. No one could get along with him.

Bill's depression is obvious in the plunging baseline of his script. Note as well the confused aspect created by the abundant altered letters, overlapping strokes, unfinished letters, and great variety of spacing and slants. All these characteristics make Bill's writing hard to read. The heaviness of his punctuation and *i* dots reinforce the notion of psychological disorder, and the tapering strokes point up his destructive tendencies. The fact that he is intelligent and quick-witted (small, speedy script) makes it obvious that Bill is aware of his psychological problems.

* * *

Monotonous Script

Henry, 62

The pressure is regular and baseline straight, yet Henry's handwriting is very monotonous. It is threadlike and impossible to read. The speed and size point up Henry's intelligence and mental agility, yet he never finished school nor took a job. He lives with his mother, who is independently wealthy.

* * *

The three samples that follow further illustrate extremely monotonous script. Monotony is a very important clue to the mental condition of the writer, as you will discover, in the detailed samples that comprise the balance of this chapter.

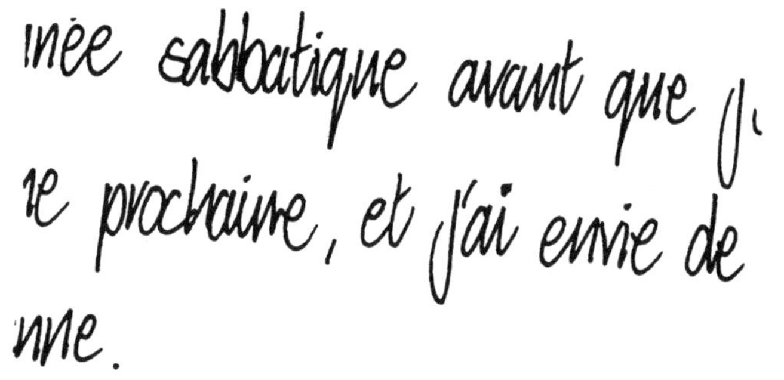
inée sabbatique avant que j'
re prochaine, et j'ai envie de
nne.

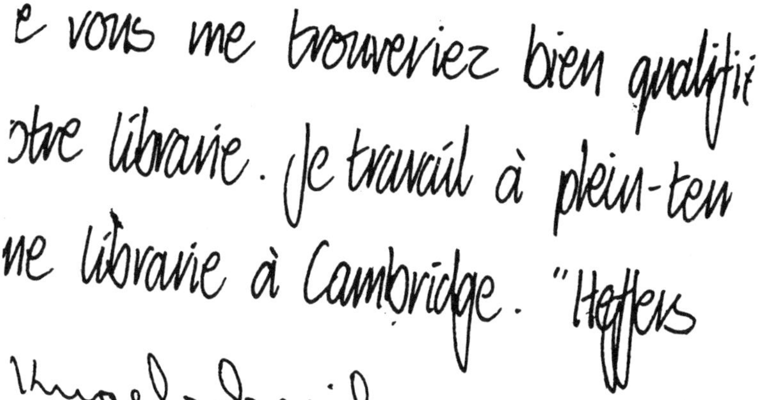
e vous me trouveriez bien qualifi
otre librairie. Je travail à plein-tem
ne librairie à Cambridge. "Heffers

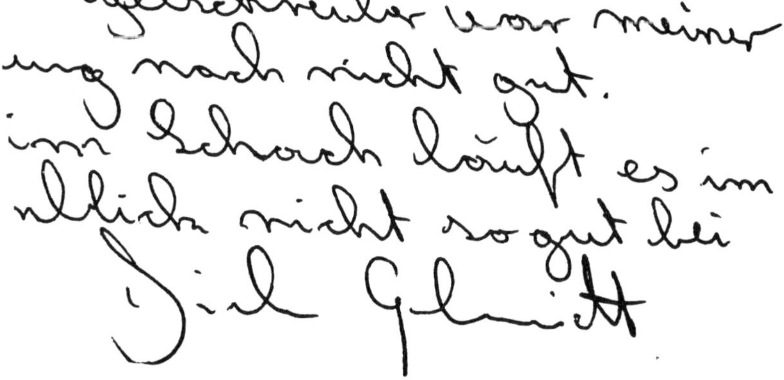
Kugelschreiber von meiner
ung nach nicht gut.
im Schach läuft es im
lich nicht so gut bei

Suite à l'invitation que vous fîtes samedi 23 s

d'étudier leur écriture, je me permets de soumei

à votre sagacité.

Je dois vous l'avouer pourtant. Sans vouloir vous

de votre aptitude à déterminer à partir de ma

mon caractère, ma libido.

* * *

Living in a Fantasy World

Here we consider a characteristic of pronounced psychological disorder. Daydreaming is common; everyone has occasional fantasies. They help us to cope with life and they exercise our imagination. People in severe mental distress, however, often adapt to their condition by fleeing reality and creating their own inner world. Consider two examples.

Simon, 27

Anbei der gewünschte Artikel von Diana Begel (— dies

hoffentlich der richtige!). Der Beitrag von Heri stammt aus einem Buch

gesagt aus seiner Habilitationsschrift) — ich werde das Literaturverzeich

kopieren. Ich habe in den letzten Tagen so viel neues Material gesami

10 Seiten schreiben müsse, um alles zu erläutern und sinngemäss einz

Togni stresst mich zusammen mit Nässle und ich

Simon lives with his parents. He can't hold on to any job because his behavior is just too odd, and he's viewed as being extremely lazy. His script is slow and looks childish and monotonous. Indeed, his intellectual evolution ended in adolescence, when he suffered a severe mental trauma.

Simon takes medication for his mental condition. He is stubborn, inhibited, and has no friends or lovers. He has escaped into his dream world, where he imagines ideal love at one extreme and debauchery at the other.

* * *

Christine, 33

Paris le 24 février 85

Bonjour,

Ici est le Rorschach-moi

Je suis Christine

Christine is delusional and has been in psychoanalysis for many years. She imagines herself to be a famous actress. She is temperamental, moody, and destructive. Note the many tapering strokes in her oversized, violent script.

Should anyone challenge Christine's fantasies or refuse to believe that she is a film star, she becomes intensely aggressive and sometimes even violent. She is totally detached from reality.

IDENTIFYING SPECIFIC PSYCHOLOGICAL PROBLEMS

Psychological disorders may develop from physical or environmental roots: a genetic predisposition, an imbalance in body chemistry, a psychological trauma, a dependence on alcohol or drugs. You and I think about psychological disorders by degrees. After all, isn't *everybody* at least a little bit "neurotic"? Yet while most of us are able to function day to day despite our mental trials, there is a minority whose abnormal behavior destroys their ability to live and to function in society—whose behavior goes beyond the neurotic. We commonly call these victims of psychological disorder "psychotic".

In practice, psychologists classify mental disorders in broad groups, ranging, for example, from mild anxiety to full-blown panic attacks; from a relatively short-term depression, arising perhaps from a personal tragedy, to long-term— even suicidal—depression that requires hospitalization and drug therapy or shock treatments. Regardless, abnormal psychological states arouse our fear and, inevitably, our fascination.

The remaining samples in this chapter offer handwriting analyses for a range of mental conditions. Like physical illness, specific psychological states are difficult to pinpoint through handwriting analysis. Remember too that the physical and the mental intertwine. We begin here with the most general characteristics of each mental disorder and proceed to specific samples.

ANXIETY/ANGUISH

Depending on your perception of what is stressful and on your reaction to prolonged stress, you may have psychological as well as physical reactions. Anxiety is a psychological product of stress, and stress contributes to anxiety, just as it may contribute to the formation of ulcers or to the cardiovascular problems described in Chapter 3. For 10 people in 100, prolonged stress and/or *perceived* stress results in an anxiety disorder: panic, obsessive-compulsive behavior, or a phobia.

These are the distinguishing graphic signs of pronounced anxiety. Examples follow.

- Speedy, difficult-to-read script.
- Extremely progressive slant—the letters almost laying, threadlike, on the baseline.
- Unfinished or omitted letters and strokes.
- Altered strokes—the letters are retouched and improved needlessly.

*   *   *

Twain, 46, is an architect, but he is not exercising his profession. He tries to do some decorating when he feels up to working.

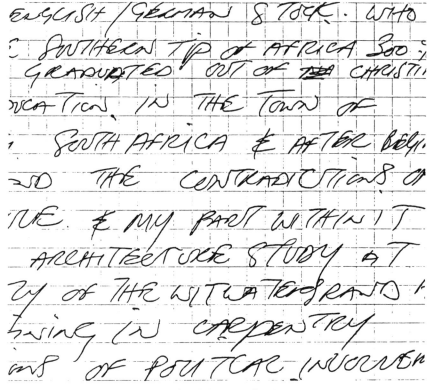

Handwriting analysis:

- Extremely irregular: emotional instability; nervous and impatient.
- Altered letters and overlapping strokes: anxiety, anguish.
- Very meandering baseline: unstable, psychotic tendencies; untrustworthy; hypocritical; a liar.
- Irregular pressure: precarious health; substance abuse.
- Strange, irregular *i* dots: psychological disorder.
- Difficult-to-read handwriting, in capital letters: confused mind; deviated emotions; psychosis.
- Superfluous dots: precarious physical health; asthma.
- Hooks: selfishness; cupidity; lying; business acumen.
- Tapering strokes: destructive tendencies.

- Reduced spacing: excessive attachment to other people; fear; anguish.
- Progressive slant: ambition; flight into the future—in this particular case.

NOTE: Depending upon the general aspect of a handwriting sample, the meaning of certain signs can show a slight variation. As your experience increases, you will be able to make the right choice and a precise final synthesis.

TWAIN'S PORTRAIT: He is intelligent, well educated, vivacious, and quick-witted. However, he is extremely nervous and impatient. His physical and his mental health are precarious. He suffers from asthma, which may have psychosomatic roots.

Twain's mind is confused. He tries to escape his responsibilities by lying and telling stories. He pretends to be working while spending most of his time sitting at home watching television or walking around aimlessly. Often he tries to find relief from anxiety in alcohol.

Twain is too self-centered to establish any kind of friendship. As often happens in psychosis, his emotions are divided. He wants friendship and love, yet his need increases his overall anxiety, and his destructive tendencies overpower his feelings. As a result, he runs away before he gets attached.

*   *   *

Jeremy, 83, is an editor and still very active in his profession. You might consider him an eccentric. Being very selfish, stubborn, and persistent, he has succeeded in achieving his professional aims, especially since he is very diplomatic and has good business sense. In his private life he was rather unlucky. If you draw his portrait, you will understand the reason.

Please send us your eat al
and quote us your on orders o
copies of chancelor press bo
(Stratford Shakespeare, Wilde, Grim

Handwriting analysis:

- Heavy *i* dots and commas: psychological disorder.
- Very meandering baseline: diplomatic; a liar.
- Fluctuating slant: emotional instability, mainly in private life; mood swings.
- Reduced speed: diplomacy; ability to conceal inner feelings and to lie.
- Garlands: selective sociability (in this case).
- Connected and disconnected script: intuitive; analytical and deductive mind.
- Coils: good business sense; attached to money.
- Very short, often tapering end strokes: destructive tendencies; neurotic; selfish.
- Altered letters: chronic anxiety; stubbornness (in this case, considering the reduced speed).
- Reduced spacing between words: selfish, egocentric person who needs affection and likes to be surrounded by people.
- Strong, regular pressure: good physical health.

*   *   *

Dick, 29, an eternal student of arts and literature:

Surprise, I imagine you weren't expecting to
from me quite so soon, but I'm never predict.
This is the best I can do for a rooftop serenade (
since I can't sing for-which) so I hope it will sit
First off, I hope your 10 page theatre paper for m
subject, si je ne trompe) is doing well — done. I too
my exam (both the written and the oral) this morning so
I feel ok about it. At least I'm pretty sure that I won't
be put in the fundamental level, which suits me fine.
Now I've got to commence rewriting my report from
this past trip, and also commence writing the one
for the trip coming up Thurs, or Friday. Not to mention
catching up in my journal. Either way, we'll see how
it goes. My family was very excited to see me and
they appreciated the postcard that I sent them a lot.
so I'm settled back in to Dijon-is life now. As a matter
of fact Paris seems about 100 years ago (it helps that I slept
for M hours last night) but I'm psyched cause I heard that
wake beat Carolina 17 to 16 saturday. Anyway, I just thought I'd
try to get a card to you before your fall break and before
your parents get to Paris. I hope church went ok yesterday,
and that you too got some rest. I've always dreamt about
running around in the streets of Paris all night long
and I wanted to thank you for putting up with me
while I did it. You were wonderful, and I had a blast.
I hope you aren't cursing my name right now, nor sick like
I am. (hello cold weather) I'm so psyched that I ran into
you in Paris! Fate or something like that. Anyway, I'm
again for a wondrous evening and the perfect finale
to a week in Paris. I'm very serious about travelling
together — one week-end to Venice. send me your schedule
and we can figure all that out. Also, I really would like

Brief analysis:

His script is excessively small and tight (avarice; meanness; selfishness; intellectual creativity; lack of maturity and assurance). The pressure and the slant are irregular (emotional instability; mood swings; psychotic tendencies; alcohol or drug abuse). The handwriting is slow (lack of honesty and reliability). Juxtaposed letters (good intuition); altered letters (anguish). There is hardly any spacing between words or lines and no margins.

DICK'S PORTRAIT: He is very immature and anxious. He hides his feelings and lies and dissembles constantly. Dick would like to be independent, but he is unable to make up his mind in what field to look for work. In fact, he is scared of taking an active approach to life, and of reality, and prefers to rely on his parents.

*   *   *

Perry, 52, formerly was an engineer, and has been in treatment for five years.

His handwriting *looks* strange. There are many sinis-trogyric, angular, and altered strokes. The *i* dots are heavy. The baseline is very meandering. The shape and the size of the letters fluctuate and change almost in every word. The pressure is irregular. The knotted loops look artificial, as do the lower loops. There are many tapering strokes.

Perry is extremely unstable and unhappy. He is unable to use his high intelligence. He does not know what he wants in life and suffers severe anxiety. His destructive tendencies are strong, and there are many contradictions in his personality.

COMPULSIVE LYING

Anxiety is the key to myriad psychological problems. Mental anguish and a sense of fear induce anxious people to begin to lie more, in order to disguise their condition or to escape the pain through flights from reality, into a fantasy world.

There are more than two dozen individual signals for lying! Earlier chapters cover this trait as well. Remember that iso-lated signs within a sample do not necessarily point to a dis-honest person. Rare indeed is the human who's never told a fib. However, when the signs accumulate to half a dozen or more, take notice: the writer lies more than the average person. Here's the complete list of strokes and signals that indicate lying:

1. Jumbled, difficult-to-read script.
2. Very meandering baseline with a light pressure.
3. Coils.
4. Extremely changing slant.
5. Sinistrogyric slant or strokes.
6. Slow, contrived script.
7. Altered letters and strokes; various shapes of the same size.
8. Jumbled but legible script.

9. Unfinished strokes or letters.
10. Threadlike script.
11. Arcades in letters or in connecting strokes.
12. Covered strokes.
13. Flourished letters.
14. Tapered strokes or letters.
15. A great variety in the sizes of the letters.
16. Improved or corrected strokes in already written words.
17. Hooks.
18. Several completely different handwritings from the same person.
19. Capital letters plunging below their normal zone.
20. End strokes of *n* or *m* reaching into the lower zone.
21. Superfluous and heavy dots in the script or at the end of the signature or the lines of address.
22. The signature or the handwritten envelope address is very different from the script of the message.
23. Odd, irregular spacing between letters.
24. Irregular speed.
25. Irregular pressure.
26. *a* and *o* open at the bottom or written with a clockwise stroke.
27. Oversized letter *I*.

*   *   *

Wendy, 33 years old, is a secretary. There are long periods when she cannot work at all.

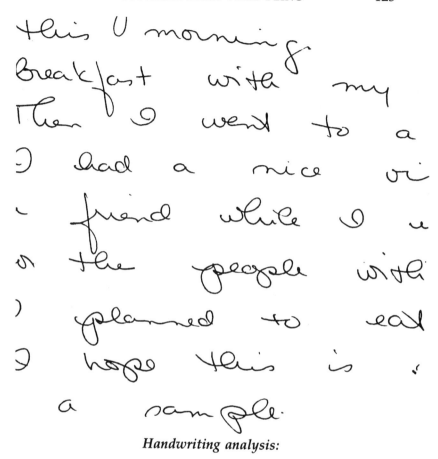

Handwriting analysis:

- Very round: affectionate and charming.
- Connected: attached to friends and family; analytical and deductive mind.
- Backward slant: problems of the past which are difficult to overcome; dissembling and lying; untrustworthy person.
- Sinistrogyric and tapering strokes: destructive tendencies; aggression; nastiness; lying.
- Sinistrogyric loops and coils: vengefulness; hypocrisy; lying.
- Threadlike letters and words: escape from reality; fear.

- Extremely wide spacing between words and lines: need for independence and freedom; the writer feels lonely and isolated—she cannot communicate.
- Concave beginning strokes: sense of humor.
- Medium to light pressure: good physical health.

NOTE: If you count the signs revealing lying you will come to six. This indicates compulsive lying, a normal phenomenon in a chronic neurosis.

WENDY'S PORTRAIT: She is very charming and feminine. Her mind is analytical and deductive. She is intelligent and has a good sense of humor.

However, Wendy is having difficulties overcoming her problems, a fact which she tries to conceal. This induces her to tell lies. She is not very happy and feels very isolated. Her aim is to escape reality by living in the past. Her personality is extremely egocentric.

Chronic anxiety prevents Wendy from working regularly and establishing satisfying relationships with other people. It is mainly her mental state which makes her untrustworthy and hypocritical.

*   *   *

Anthony, 27, studies literature and works part time at different jobs. He is a compulsive liar.

Dear Claude,

Why have you not written? ... reach you in New York and nothing since. Hope this finds with you and yours.

Has been a hectic year for fittingly by spending the h under ... touring New Z stopovers in Sydney and I Do write and been doing.

P.S. New home address:

Handwriting analysis:

- Medium to small size: intelligent, quick witted, vivacious.
- Angular and round shapes: mature, intellectual.
- Very irregular slant: mood swings; temper tantrums; mental instability; neurotic tendencies.
- Tapering strokes: aggressive and nasty.
- Hooks, coils, and sinistrogyric ringlets: business acumen; cupidity; diplomacy; lying; untrustworthy person.
- Altered strokes and letters: the writer can lie and dissemble out of fear and anxiety; neurosis; chronic depression.

- Reduced, ink-filled vowels: the writer feels frustrated in materialistic pleasures; he suffers from lack of money.
- Heavy *i* dots of various shapes: chronic neurosis; depression; unstable moods; frustration.
- Angular, sinistrogyric strokes: vengefulness; destructive tendencies; aggression.
- Knotted and angular lower loops: materialistic and sexual frustrations; inner violence; selfishness.
- Reduced, often tapering, end strokes: selfish person; lack of feelings for other people; avaricious person.
- Speedy: intelligence; good education; the writer is witty, clever, and very cunning.
- Wide and irregular spacing between words: independence; loneliness; the writer has difficulties in establishing relationships with other people. He feels isolated.

NOTE: Count the signs which indicate lying: coils, hooks, tapering strokes, altered letters written in various shapes, sinistrogyric strokes, heavy *i* dots, various slants, flourished capital letters. They number eight in all.

PORTRAIT OF ANTHONY: He is intelligent and well educated. His mind is quick, analytical, and deductive. He has a good business sense. However, his destructive tendencies and his mood swings are too strong to enable him to have a steady aim in life and to achieve his goals. Anthony suffers from chronic depression. He is not happy.

His personality is extremely self-centered, egocentric, and unstable. He is constantly lying and dissembling and thereby encountering difficulties in communicating with other people. In spite of his intelligence and his wit, he is too selfish to have any close friends. He is very lonely and feels frustrated in all fields.

*   *   *

Fred, 26, an art student, vacillates between painting and writing. He has been in psychoanalysis for many years. Like Anthony in the preceding sample, Fred is highly intelligent yet anxious and has problems with relationships.

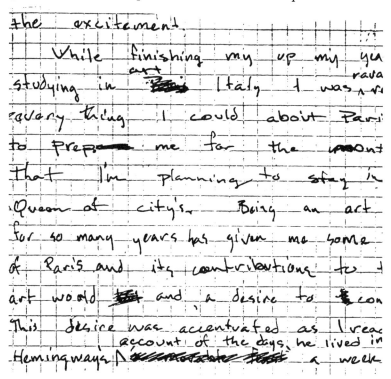

Brief analysis:

We have here a very meandering baseline (emotional instability); altered letters (anguish); extremely wide spacing (loneliness, independence); irregular pressure (psychotic tendencies, alcohol abuse); slow and sinistrogyric script (hypocrisy, untrustworthiness); lack of end strokes (selfishness, meanness); fluctuating slant (mood swings); small size (intelligence, virility).

There are nine signs revealing lying: meandering baseline, altered letters, overlapping strokes, fluctuating slant, coils, heavy *i* dots, hooks, sinistrogyric strokes, unfinished letters.

FRED'S PORTRAIT: Though intelligent and certainly creative, Fred is extremely unstable, anxious, and lonely. Since he constantly changes his life plan and his goals, he is unable to complete his education. Fred often feels depressed and indolent. He avoids taking any responsibility for himself or others.

With this general childish, self-centered attitude, it's obvious that Fred is immature. He also lacks a sense of graciousness toward other people. He finds it difficult to reveal himself to others, and this feeds his lying, which already has become a compulsion.

CRUELTY

Often cruelty is induced by mental suffering. When we can't cope, we may get angry and take our anger out on others, as if by hurting them we can help ourselves. Certainly this does not excuse all inhumane behavior, but it may point to one cause and, thereby, to its correction.

At the extreme are those remorseless few whom psychologists call antisocial personalities—sociopaths or psychopaths to you and me. Antisocial personalities seem to have no feeling for others and to fear nothing. They lie, cheat, and steal without remorse. They have no conscience. When they possess as well a high degree of intelligence, sociopaths may become cool, charming, and clever con artists.

While sociopaths may be criminals, the vast majority of criminals are *not* sociopaths, for despite their antisocial behavior, most criminals do show care and concern at least for friends and family.

To pick up on the trait of cruelty, look for the following signs in the handwriting:

- Monotonous script.
- Tight spacing.
- Sticklike script.
- Tapering strokes; reduced end strokes.
- Heavy, often angular, *i* dots.

* * *

Betty, 27, is a student of literature and languages. She is selfish, cruel, and childish—a spoiled brat!

s, thus, of a high standard but I wanted
a period, immediately after my degree
fluency. In studying french Literature
Parisian life from a literary stance and
to realise this, especially because of Paris'
ultural centre.
Open my own bookstore in Britain within
's as there are many small business
? if you are under twenty-five years of age.

Brief analysis:

Her script looks monotonous (psychotic tendencies, cruelty). It is very slow and does not look natural (hypocrisy; a liar). The middle zone is pronounced (attachment to money; need for immediate gratification; selfishness), with tight spacing (avarice; selfishness). The shapes are very round (need for affection; immaturity and childish behavior). Reduced end strokes (lack of generosity; the writer is economically inclined).

* * *

Frank, 27, spends his time making plans for the future but cannot finish any task. He keeps changing his plans. You should have no problems drawing a portrait of Frank.

> and what I am going to make of my futu
> fond of everything expressive, and so I
> little acting, singing, painting, dancing, photo
> writing and playing the guitarre. I'm not
> good at any of these things but I've tric
> all. The problem is that society demands
> tion and proffesionalism and [crossed out] I dou´
> like choosing. It's like when we travel we
> have to go to some place ispecifik. I see t
> as a goal in itself. Maybe I will find.

Handwriting analysis:

- Monotonous: psychological disorder; immaturity.
- Sticklike: aggressive and violent; nasty, cruel, and selfish.
- Slow and artificial: untrustworthy; immature.
- Angular, sinistrogyric strokes in the lower loops: regressive, vengeful libido.
- Tight spacing: greedy; extremely attached to others.
- Absence of end strokes: selfish and stingy.

* * *

Arthur, 46, is in prison for life. He was a professional thief; the content of his sample reveals it. Arthur raped and killed four small boys at different times and in two different states before being caught and convicted. His handwriting is typical and shows all the signs of a dangerous criminal who should be in psychiatric treatment. Let's analyze his script in detail.

Handwriting analysis:

- Small and fast, round and angular: very high intelligence; good education; quick mind; vivacious; mature.
- Fluctuating slant: emotional instability; mental problems.
- Strange, sometimes wavy, irregular lower loops: fluctuating libido; sexual ambivalence; unfaithfulness; instability; deviated emotions.
- Altered letters: unreliability; lying; anguish; flight from reality.
- Irregular pressure: mental problems; deviated emotions; poor health.

- Overlapping, sinistrogyric strokes: lying; hypocrisy; dissembling; selfish; sly person.
- Tight script: self-centered, avaricious, greedy person; deviated feelings of guilt.
- Arcades: lying; hypocrisy; arrogance.
- Lack of end strokes: selfishness; avarice.
- Heavy *i* dots: schizophrenic tendencies.
- Meandering baseline: untrustworthy.
- Tapering strokes: destructive tendencies.
- Strange, falsely improved letters: anxiety; anguish; hypocrisy.
- Ink-filled vowels and loops: sexual fantasies; lying; ambivalent libido, debauchery.

PORTRAIT OF ARTHUR: His emotions are deviated, his personality contradictory. On the one hand, his intelligence and level of maturity are high. Yet his feelings, emotions, and sexuality are stunted. He seems to be trying to escape reality by living in his fantasies.

Arthur has no morals or principles. He does not believe in earning a living and simply takes what he wants without regard to anyone. If he encounters any opposition, he uses violence. To say that he is self-centered and avaricious is putting it mildly. Since he is sexually attracted to young children, the dangers are obvious.

Strangely, Arthur does experience feelings of guilt, but these feelings center only on his fantasies. For his real, horrific crimes he feels no guilt and no regret!

* * *

Boris, 44, works irregularly. He is an architect. His cruelty surfaces frequently, and he directs it toward people and toward animals. He has a vicious temper. It would not be too strong to label Boris an antisocial personality.

Brief analysis:

Note the pronounced middle zone in his extremely large, angular, tapering script. The script has a tight appearance, with reduced end strokes, numerous hooks and coils, and overlapping and regressive strokes. The pressure is heavy, as are the angular *i* dots.

Even as an amateur graphologist, the violence in this script should be evident to you. Boris is aggressive, sly, vindictive, and very selfish.

DEPRESSION

Who hasn't been depressed? Depression vies with anxiety as the most commonly experienced mental problem. Perhaps one-fifth of women and one-tenth of men will experience a major depression at some time during their lives.

It's difficult to draw the line between life's normal "downs" and the extremes of depression that qualify as full-blown psychological disorders. A clue lies in the cause of the depression. Deep sadness is an appropriate response to a tragedy, such as the loss of a loved one. Yet if a bout with depression seems to drag on and on *without* any apparent reason, major depression should be the suspect.

The symptoms of depression of any degree include insomnia, loss of energy and interest in anyone or anything, feelings of worthlessness, and loss of appetite. In the handwriting, the following signs will appear:

- Suddenly the baseline will plunge downward.
- Individual letters, garlands, and end zones tend to fall below their appropriate zone.
- Irregular spacing and pressure.
- Altered, unfinished letters which are difficult to read.
- Sinistrogyric, open lower loops.
- Ink-filled letters, especially vowels.
- Tapering strokes.
- Overlapping strokes.

*   *   *

Reactional Depression

As its name implies, this category of depression has a cause: Reactional depression is an appropriate response to aversive life events. While the most severe cases (losing a spouse, for example) may last over a year, eventually the depression lifts and the person overcomes the tragedy and gets on with life, as the following samples illustrate.

*   *   *

Jim, 37 and an engineer, is an only child and very attached to his mother, who died a month ago. Since, as you will note in analyzing his handwriting, all the signs of depression are present in a rather mild form, it seems that Jim will bounce back from his depression within a reasonable time.

Claude,

I hope you're finding New York exciting and that you are in good health and spirit. Happy to hear that Joe and Danny are getting along well and hopefully he has taken you to all the sites. Have you found that sushi bar by Cooper Square - There is a very fine engineering college on

Handwriting analysis:

- Very meandering baseline, plunging downward: the writer is depressed and very unhappy; his feelings are unstable.
- Altered, unfinished letters which are difficult to read: the person tries to hide his mental sufferings; he conceals his feelings and lies to protect himself.
- Sinistrogyric, open lower loops: sexual problems; reduced and ambivalent libido and energy level.

- Ink-filled letters and vowels: the writer's attachment to his mother was excessive; he's living in a fantasy world.
- Irregular spacing and pressure: emotional instability; deviated emotions.
- Tapering strokes: destructive tendencies; nastiness.
- Overlapping strokes: dishonesty; lying.

* * *

Jerry, an English teacher, is 43 years old. He lost his only son in a car accident and is deeply depressed, as his brief sample reveals.

Handwriting analysis:

- Downward-plunging baseline: depression.
- Extremely meandering baseline: mood swings.
- Certain letters plunging suddenly below the baseline: depression.
- Angular, tapering, and sinistrogyric strokes: vengefulness; destructive tendencies; nastiness.
- Launching upward endings: temper tantrums.
- Altered, difficult-to-read letters: the writer tries to hide his feelings and lies.

- Irregular spacing and pressure: deviated emotions; anguish; depression.
- Lack of end strokes: selfishness.

* * *

Philip, a 29-year-old medical student, was very attached to his girlfriend. She left all of a sudden and married a much older businessman. In time, Philip will overcome his depression.

> Dear Claude,
>
> here I am sitting in a Parisian book store writing absolute rubbish for a hand-writing test. An obnoxious frenchman is trying to divert my attention by asking me the meaning of 'wobble.' Something my brain appears

Handwriting analysis:

- The baseline and some individual letters are plunging downward: depression and despair.
- Irregular pressure: deviated emotions; lack of courage.
- Very meandering baseline: inner instability; the person feels insecure.
- Open, tapering, and sinistrogyric lower loops: regressive libido; destructive tendencies.

- Heavy *i* dots: deviated emotions; mental suffering; depression.
- Altered letters with overlapping strokes: the person hides his suffering; he lies and conceals his feelings.

* * *

Willy, a journalist who is 38, worked for many years in the news division of a major television network. While he was on assignment in Europe, he lost his job as a result of a power struggle in the home office. Naturally, his response to these unexpected events included a severe reactional depression. Willy firmly believes that he will never again find an interesting job, and he's becoming more and more pessimistic. He's putting on a brave face, pretending to take it in stride, but it's all a front.

As you can see, his script is difficult to read, with altered and tapering letters. Some words are threadlike. The slant becomes sinistrogyric, and the baseline droops down. The pressure is still regular and strong, however. Sooner or later, Willy will overcome his depression.

* * *

Markus, 28, gave up his studies and his part-time job to become a professional chessplayer. He regrets his decision: He cannot earn his living by playing chess, and it's too late for him to become an International Master.

The great many altered letters and overlapping strokes in Markus's script reveal his inner anxiety. However, as his handwriting still shows a rather firm pressure and is readable, this young man likely will overcome his depression and find a job he likes.

In this sample you will notice once more the many heavy *i* dots as well as some superfluous dots. The handwriting is very slow. As happens in most depressions, the baseline is plunging downwards.

London.

Dear. Claude.

I enjoyed our chess game. of. Sunday past. Perhapse you will return to the manhattan. Chess Club. again. Hope to See. You soon.

* * *

Mary-Ann, 24, lived with her parents while she attended college. Last semester she failed all her exams, and her parents reproached her for being lazy and too involved in her social life. As a result, Mary-Ann left home.

> Jout !
>
> in a few times befor
> when I can recite poetr
> t caddying (remember me)
> f June 20-27 is the

Handwriting analysis:

- Altered script: anxiety; fear and anguish; depression.
- Overlapping strokes: the writer conceals her feelings and can lie; deviated emotions.
- Very slow, disconnected writing: lack of maturity; dishonesty; hypocrisy; stubbornness.
- Heavy *i* dots: emotional problems; depression.
- Changing slant: mood swings.
- Abrupt endings: selfishness.
- Tapering strokes: destructive tendencies.
- Baseline droops downward: depression.
- Irregular pressure: emotional instability; deviated emotions.

PORTRAIT OF MARY-ANN: All the signs in her script reveal a

pronounced reactional depression as well as a lack of maturity and limited intelligence. Mary-Ann was not very happy in her home life, yet now that she's on her own, she feels isolated. Her inner strength is limited, as is her dynamism, and she is rather stubborn.

Her disposition represents to me a borderline case between temporary, reactional depression and the psychological disorder called "major depression," which we'll cover next.

* * *

Major Depression

When depression lasts for weeks or more without apparent cause, it's reasonable to suspect a major depression. While it's been observed that most major depressions last fewer than three months and most people rebound to normal without professional help, it's also true that about half of those who recover will suffer another episode within two years. Enduring recovery from depression seems linked to low stress and consistent social support.

Indicative of its chronic nature, you will note in the following samples the development of a monotonous aspect in the script of people suffering major depression.

* * *

Heinz, 47, organizes sporting and leisure events. He works only part time and has been in psychoanalytic treatment for more than twenty years. Note especially the monotony in his writing and the plunging baseline.

Handwriting analysis:

- Extremely monotonous aspect: psychological disorder.
- Steadily downward-plunging baseline: depression.
- Tight spacing and connected script: extreme attachment to friends; fear of being alone.
- Heavy *i* dots: psychological problems; depression.
- Overlapping strokes: the writer is dissembling and can lie.
- Coils: business acumen; diplomacy; hypocrisy; lying.
- Knotted loops: persistence; stubbornness (in his case).
- Covered strokes in several vowels: egocentric person; narcissism.

* * *

Nigel, 36, is not working. His parents support him. He refuses psychoanalysis and prefers to travel.

> I will send this to Shakey's in the hope that you drop in there occasionally. I hope things are going good for you in Paris. It would be so good to see you again. Who knows. Please, I'm praying that you'll write

Handwriting analysis:

- Monotonous: chronic depression.
- Extremely irregular, wide spacing: the writer is very independent and lonely.
- Heavy, irregular *i* dots: neurotic tendencies.
- Slow writing: immaturity; low intelligence; mental blockade at the age of adolescence; lack of intellectual evolution.
- Sticklike strokes: nastiness; contained aggression.
- Overlapping strokes: dishonesty; lying.
- Open loops in the lower zone: sexual ambivalence.

BRIEF PORTRAIT OF NIGEL: He is extremely immature. The monotonous aspect of his script indicates his chronic suffering. Nigel is not very happy; he has difficulties in communicating and suffers from loneliness. He has no relationships with women.

* * *

Miriam, 52, has been in treatment and takes lithium. Her condition is stabilized (straight baseline). She is rather lonely and has never been married. She is not working and lives with her parents.

Dear Claude,

I'm not at all convinced by this. For example my 'S'. This is the worst of a change of school at the age of 10 who insisted I try to

EATING DISORDERS

Psychologists view eating disorders mainly as a cultural phenomenon. Anorexia and bulimia occur far more often in women than in men, and exclusively in Western societies with weight-obsessed standards of beauty, where "fat is bad" and "thin is beautiful."

Research has shown that those diagnosed with anorexia, a disorder in which the person starves herself yet still feels fat, often come from overprotective parents or families of high achievers. Bulimics, or closet eaters, who tend to fluctuate around a normal weight level often are successful at keeping their binge/purge episodes hidden. According to research, families of bulimia patients characteritically have high incidences of alcoholism, obesity, and/or depression.

The graphic signs of eating disorders include:

- Tight spacing; no margins.
- Threadlike script.
- Coils in the vowels.
- Unfinished strokes hanging in midair may signal anorexia.
- Pronounced middle zone with very round shapes points to a "closet eater," or bulimic.

* * *

Martha, 43, lives with her parents and works sporadically at a variety of odd jobs, such as babysitting, the local flea market, cooking for special occasions, and so forth.

Handwriting analysis:

- Extremely monotonous: psychological disorder; stubbornness.
- Very slow and childish looking: lack of intellectual maturity; stalled at adolescence.
- Sinistrogyric slant: flight from reality into the past; incapacity to overcome problems and assume responsibilities; lying and dissembling; stubbornness.
- Round, regular shapes: great need for affection; feminine charm.
- Pronounced middle zone: need for immediate gratification; selfishness; immaturity.
- Arcades, mainly in *m*'s and *n*'s: ability to manipulate others; selfishness.
- Heavy *i* dots: psychological problems.
- Wide spacing between words: independence; loneliness.
- Weak, small, and open lower loops: regressive libido.
- Medium, regular pressure: good physical health.
- Baseline plunging slightly downward: depression.
- Absence of margins: self-centered and childish person.
- Regressive hooks and coils: selfishness; lying; attachment to money; business acumen.
- Juxtaposed script: good intuition; independence.

MARTHA'S PORTRAIT: A psychiatrist might say that Martha is fixated at the oral stage of development. Her need for immediate gratification is excessive. If it's unfulfilled, she becomes depressed, and her depressions can last for weeks.

Martha can make life miserable for those around her. She is very stubborn and not easily coaxed into action. She doesn't believe in working hard and has no ambitions or goals. Being completely egocentric, she sees others as important only if she can manipulate them to get what she wants. She has no close relationships and no regard for other people.

* * *

Ondine, 33, is incapable of working or studying. She lives with her parents and travels. She is in psychoanalysis.

> 15.45
>
> Dear George—
> Thank you for letting me stay. Perhaps is it OK if I stay again or around the middle of march? I enjoyed reading sections in Anaïs Nin about you, and I was wishing you'd be here when I left. Anyway, thank you.
>
> Love, Ondine

Handwriting analysis:

- Extremely meandering baseline: mental instability; lies out of fear and anxiety.
- Changing slant: mood swings; untrustworthy.
- Heavy *i* dots: psychological disorder.
- Baseline plunges downward: depressive moods: neurosis.
- Coils in most vowels: egocentric behavior; narcissism: excessive masturbation; eating disorders.

BRIEF PORTRAIT OF ONDINE: Her psychological problems date back to her childhood. She is emotionally unstable, lonely, and very unhappy. Ondine is self-centered and untrustworthy. It's nearly impossible for her to make a friend.

EMOTIONAL INSTABILITY

Mood swings are a near-ubiquitous characteristic of psychological disorder. The samples in this section represent an extreme range of emotional instability, from mood swings of anxious, neurotic people to full-blown manic-depressive disorder, in which the afflicted person vacillates among deep depression, brief periods of lucidity, and the euphoric, hyperactive, wildly optimistic state of mania. During the manic phase, the person is loud, flighty, grandiose, and has little need for sleep. Manics may show few sexual inhibitions, and their elation easily turns to irritation if they are crossed. Often, they need to be protected from themselves.

Manic-depressive psychosis, or bipolar disorder as the psychologists call it, is relatively rare, occurring in less than one percent of the U.S. population. In its milder forms, the energy, sensitivity, and free-flowing creativity of mania can fuel the work of artists, writers, and poets, as we shall see.

Added to the graphic signs of depression, the characteristic script of manics include the following:

- The baseline meanders. Typically, the more extreme the meandering, the more intense the disorder.
- A variety of slants in a single sample.

* * *

Perry, 52, the former owner of a small bookshop, is not working anymore.

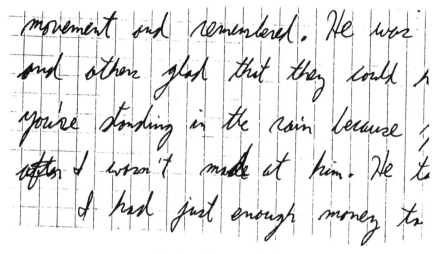

Handwriting analysis:

- Extremely meandering baseline: emotional instability; lying; untrustworthy; psychological disorders.
- Great variety of shapes, altered letters: hypocrisy; lying; the writer conceals his feelings; fear of reality; anxious; untrustworthy.
- Unfinished letters: timid; susceptible; the writer is very sensitive.
- Various-sized letters: emotional instability; mood swings; the writer lacks maturity and self-confidence.
- Hooks and covered strokes: the writer is cunning and sly; business acumen; hypocrisy; lying and dissembling.
- Lack of end strokes: selfishness; the writer is economical.
- Some *a*'s and *o*'s written in a clockwise direction contrary to the normal counterclockwise stroke: untrustworthy; lying; ability to steal.
- Connected script: attached to other people.

- Heavy and strange *i* dots and periods: psychological disorder.
- Round and angular strokes: intelligent; mature.
- Progressive slant: optimistic; ambitious.
- Very irregular speed: emotional instability; immaturity.

PERRY'S PORTRAIT: He is intelligent and has a quick, lively mind, but his personality is extremely contradictory. He is ambitious and optimistic and at the same time timid, unstable, and not very sure of himself. Considering his age, Perry lacks maturity. He has some business sense; however, his mood swings and his inner instability prevent him from achieving his goals.

Perry never finishes the tasks he begins. He is very impatient and selfish. He is afraid of other people and of reality. Therefore he prefers to live in a fantasy world woven of lies. This makes him untrustworthy and hypocritical. He can be influenced easily and is tempted to steal.

*   *   *

Andrew, 37, works at various jobs. He does not have any particular profession. Andrew's psychological problems are chronic. He is on the border between neurosis and psychosis.

grew up in Florida
left U.S.A in 1984
lived in Switzerland, W. Germany,
Paris and travelled the most
of Europe for two years.
Returned to Paris in

Handwriting analysis:

- Disconnected, extremely slow, and awkward: immaturity; low intelligence; lying; untrustworthiness.
- Altered letters: anxiety; anguish; lying out of fear.
- Covered strokes: dissembling and lying.
- Very meandering baseline: emotional instability; diplomacy; lying.
- Fluctuating slant: mood swings; emotional instability; psychological disorder.
- Heavy and strange *i* dots and commans: neurosis.
- Tapering strokes: destructive tendencies.
- Lack of end strokes: selfishness; greed.
- Irregular pressure: substance abuse; bad health.
- Wide, irregular spacing: independence; loneliness.

*   *   *

Maude is 55 and a victim of manic-depressive psychosis. In her youth, the disorder forced her to leave college in order to undergo treatment. Like so many with this disorder, Maude is highly intelligent. The tragedy is that her alternating agitation and depression leave little room for her to exercise her gifts or to concentrate at all.

Cardiovascular disease is often the result of successive bouts of mania. You can see the signs in Maude's handwriting.

Brief analysis:

- Very meandering, downward-plunging baseline: emotional instability; depression; lying; poor health.
- Altered, difficult-to-read letters: anguish; emotional instability; lying and dissembling; psychological disorder.
- Individual letters plunging below the baseline: acute depression; unreliability.
- Wide spacing, isolated letters: independence; loneliness; mental problems.
- Unfinished strokes and letters: anxiety; anguish.

* * *

Vladimir Maiakovsky was a Russian playwright. His best-known work is "The Bedbug." As we observed earlier in the analysis of Hemingway, it's not as a rule beneficial to the beginner to study the script of celebrated artists, for they are exceptional people whose mental suffering finds relief in their masterpieces. However, Maiakovsky's case offers a poignant example of the effects of hardship on the psyche.

Maiakovsky celebrated the Russian revolution, but its outcome disappointed him. He was persecuted by Stalin and prevented from writing and publishing his work. He committed suicide in Leningrad in 1930. The following sample was written at age 36, shortly before his death.

Handwriting analysis:

- Overlapping strokes: inner anxiety and dissembling; diplomacy.
- Baseline plunges at the right margin: depression; physical and mental ailments.
- Altered letters: the person can lie and dissemble out of fear; anguish.
- Sinistrogyric strokes: inner suffering from past problems; dissembling.
- Certain letters are plunging too far below the baseline: depression; mental disorder.
- Many ink-filled vowels: deviated emotions; fantasies of debauchery; destructive tendencies.
- Underlined words and lines: psychotic tendencies; anguish; flight from reality; self-destructive tendencies; difficulties in communicating with other people.
- Fast and small writing: high intelligence; good education; virility; intellectual creativity.
- Concave beginning strokes: sense of humor.

BRIEF PORTRAIT OF VLADIMIR MAIAKOVSKY: He was very intelligent and creative, with an analytical and deductive mind. But he lived mainly within his fantasies and had trouble adjusting to reality. As a result, his destructive tendencies took the upper hand. His sense of the comic was superb, yet his chronic depression increased over time. (It is surprising to note how many humorists commit suicide.)

The continuing ban on his work increased his mental disorder and his economic deprivation. The authorities failed to grasp his genius despite the success of his plays. Maiakovsky's private life and his social network fell apart as a result of his inner turmoil and his political ostracism. He died a lonely and isolated man.

* * *

NOTE: profoundly disturbed people may choose to say no to life *not* at moments of extreme agitation, as you might think. Rather, the most dangerous periods come when the person is in the throes of the deepest depression and appears completely immobile.

EMOTIONAL WITHDRAWAL

To protect themselves from intolerable circumstances—either real or imaginary—some people withdraw from reality. Among the graphic signals of emotional withdrawal are the following:

- Irregular and very wide spacing.
- Capital letters are disconnected from the script and may show a backward slant.
- Discordant and altered letters. On the same page, for example, the writer will use half a dozen different shapes to represent the letter *a*.

Among the most uncommon and mysterious forms of emotional withdrawal is the phenomenon of multiple personality. This involves the separation of self from ordinary consciousness via the unconscious development of two or more distinct personalities. One personality may be restrained and inhibited; the other impulsive and boisterous. Each personality has its own mannerisms, including a separate voice, and the original personality typically is unaware of the existence of the other(s).

*   *   *

Stanley, 46, has spent many years in mental institutions. He is currently in prison for armed assault. He does not remember his crime. He has two separate personalities and, not surprisingly, two separate handwritings.

BRIEF ANALYSIS: Both of Stanley's samples show altered, discordant letters (check the *a*'s). The heavy *i* dots reveal his mental disorder, and the tapering strokes his inner violence and aggression. He is incapable of communicating his feelings. He is insecure and wants companionship and help for his suffering.

In the first sample, the extremely wide spacing reveals the loneliness of the writer. In the second the entangled letters and tight spacing between the lines indicate that this personality "Sidney," craves companionship and affection.

PROBLEMS WITH RELATIONSHIPS

- Wide spacing and juxtaposed script may indicate that the writer avoids intimacy.
- Tight spacing and very connected, round script may signal the opposite; a person who can't separate himself or herself from others.

*   *   *

Helen, 39, has been working as a graphic designer in a public relations firm.

Dear Clarke,

This morning

up early to get 7

meeting on holiday.

While I was there

Handwriting analysis:

- Very large: feminine; ambitious; high, idealistic goals; megalomania.
- Altered letters, great variety of shapes: confused mind; emotional instability.
- Violent tapering strokes: destructive tendencies; aggression; inner violence.
- Very high upper stems: megalomania; the aims are higher than the person's abilities; vanity.

- Very reduced shapes in the lower zone: regressive libido.
- Strange, often absent, *i* dots: psychological disorder.
- Strange spacing between words: deviated emotions; psychosis.
- Gap separating the initial letter of each phrase: problems with parents.

HELEN'S PORTRAIT: She is feminine and dynamic, but her mind is confused and illogical. These constraints prevent her from achieving her lofty goals. Helen has a narcissistic personality: She thinks of herself as a talented artist and fantasizes about her unlimited success while overreacting mightily to any sort of criticism. Her frustrations, inner instability, and destructive tendencies are overwhelming her.

Although her sex drive is reduced, Helen nevertheless believes herself to be irresistible. She invents strange stories (including one about being a famous actress) in order to impress, and her act is very convincing. When newfound friends learn the truth about Helen, they abandon her, and this contributes to her instability.

Helen is lonely and unable to adjust to real life. If you count the signals for lying in her script, you will come to eight—hooks; tapering strokes; altered letters; overlapping strokes; angular *i* dots; sinistrogyric strokes (use your magnifying glass); excessively high stems; embellished capital letters.

* * *

Ken, 39, is a journalist and has the talent to become an established writer. Once again, use a magnifying glass to analyze this sample. Even if you don't read French, you will have no problems interpreting the script. Ken's high intelligence makes his writing more difficult to analyze than the average, but the effort will help you to progress in your proficiency.

Chère Madame,

Je vous prie d'excuser le retard
vous répondre : faute de moins en
temps disponible ! Je regrette de
me rendre à la soirée - signatures
J'ai lu une partie du Marché et
j'y préfère votre style de nouvelliste
précise, je suis intraitable : vous ne
voit ! J'
Meilleurs vœux pour 1990
Amitiés

Handwriting analysis:

- Small and fast: high intelligence; quick mind; vivacious; mature; virile.
- Connected and juxtaposed: good education; intellectual creativity; sociable; mature.
- Wide spacing between words: independence; loneliness.
- Light, irregular pressure: impatience; changing aims; emotional instability; nervousness.
- Heavy *i* dots and punctuation: psychological problems.
- Altered letters and various shapes: emotional instability; moodiness; acute diplomacy; lying; anguish.
- Very meandering baseline: emotional instability; nervousness; lying; untrustworthiness; unreliability; hypocrisy; psychological disorder.
- Normal, closed lower loops: heterosexual libido.
- Lack of end strokes: selfishness; parsimony; meanness.
- Certain vowels are made of clockwise strokes and open at

the bottom: unreliability; the person can lie and dissemble; the writer can be tempted to steal; disordered reasoning and behavior.

KEN'S PORTRAIT: Since his mind is so sharp, he has little patience for the intellectual struggles of others. He finds it hard to communicate his own feelings and lacks any regard for the feelings of others. He has married several times, but only briefly. Even as he pushes others away, Ken struggles with his own great need for affection. He is terribly lonely. His selfishness, inner instability, and psychotic tendencies are increasing.

Ken is certain that he will become a famous author as soon as his first novel is published. He started it some twenty years ago. He hardly ever finishes what he starts. His aims are forever changing, and he lacks conviction and persistence. His anxiety induces him to make up stories, and he's difficult to trust. If you make him a loan, you'll never see your money again.

REGRESSIVE LIBIDO

Remember, in graphology the libido refers to attitude, energy level, and willpower as well as to sexuality. You will note the following aspects in the script:

- Monotonous aspect; sinistrogyric slant.
- Light, weak, sometimes irregular pressure.
- Lower stems and loops are often open, hanging down limply into the lower zone. The stems seem to be melting away.
- Weak, imprecise *t* crossings.

* * *

Jill, 35, lives with her mother. She does not work.

Handwriting analysis:

- Very monotonous: psychological disorder.
- Sinistrogyric slant: living in the past; immaturity and stunted intellectual development; flight from reality; romanticism; lying; untrustworthy; egocentric, selfish person; lazy.
- Round, with angular back-slanting strokes in the lower loops: great need for affection; regressive and vengeful libido; needs immediate materialistic gratification; selfish; lazy; lacks ambition.
- Heavy *i* dots placed to the left of the stem: psychological disorder.
- Covered strokes: hypocrisy; dissembling.
- Lacks end strokes: selfish, self-centered person who tends to be very economical or stingy.
- Arcades in the *m*'s and *n*'s: arrogance; no respect for others.
- Wide spacing between words: need for independence and solitude.

- Tight spacing between letters: selfish; extremely attached to parents; greedy.

JILL'S PORTRAIT: In spite of her age, Jill is extremely attached to her mother; she cannot conceive of living without her. Her aim is to remain childlike and to live in the past. She is lazy and interested only in immediate gratification. She tries to hide her anxiety about the future.

Because she is very self-centered, it is difficult for Jill to establish relationships. She lies constantly and tries to exploit and manipulate others. Her feelings are romantic, but her intellectual and psychological evolution stopped at the age of sixteen. She is very feminine but also childish, inhibited, and immature.

At the present time she is in psychoanalysis. However, as she is very stubborn, there is little change in her personality. She suffers from chronic depression. Her father has been in a mental hospital for many years.

*   *   *

Fred, 33, is not working, despite his university teaching. He is in psychoanalytic treatment, and when he feels well, he travels. Considering his inability to work and to function day-to-day, he is a disabled person.

at Eton College, and in am de taking my A-levels in French, Maths. Hence an Literature shop in France an ideal opportunity for me much of what I have lea

Handwriting analysis:

- Extremely monotonous: psychological disorder; immaturity.
- Regressive slant: living in the past; no ambition and no desires; selfish.
- Threadlike letters: fear of reality; diplomacy; lying and dissembling.
- Garlands: desire to communicate; attached to his friends.
- Tapering, sinistrogyric strokes: destructive tendencies.
- Round shapes and large, regressive lower loops: sexual ambivalence; homosexual tendencies; emotional instability.
- Very regular, wide spacing: independent; lonely.
- Very weak *t* crossings: lack of willpower and strength.
- Irregular, rather weak pressure: precarious mental health.

FRED'S PORTRAIT: He is intelligent and well educated but feels very unhappy and bored. He has no aims and no goals in life. Rather timid and shy, Fred tries to escape reality by living in the past.

His personality is very weak. His lying stems from anxiety. Like most mentally disordered people, Fred lives in a fantasy world and makes up stories. This minimizes his trustworthiness. He lacks willpower, maturity, and virility. He is afraid of people and especially of men, in spite of his latent homosexuality.

Three times a week he sees a psychiatrist. Along with his chronic anxiety, Fred's destructive and self-destructive tendencies contribute to his chronic depression.

*   *   *

Fernando, 29, has worked in various jobs: as a salesman, an electrician, a cashier in a bank among many others. He usually gets fired within a short time.

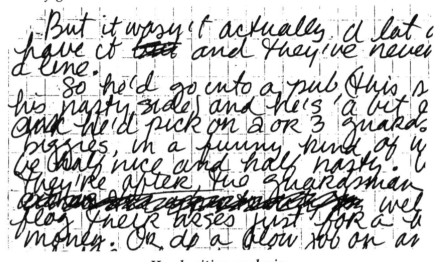

Handwriting analysis:

- Confused script: confused mind, immature and illogical.
- Tight spacing: mental confusion; extreme attachment to people stemming from anxiety and anguish; lack of independence; avarice.
- Extremely strong pressure: inner feelings of aggression and violence; weak personality.
- Numerous capital letters in the middle of words: psychological disorder.
- Altered letters and words: anxiety; anguish; hypocrisy; lies out of fear.
- Slow script: limited intellectual abilities; hypocrisy.
- Tapering strokes: destructive tendencies; lying.
- Extremely round shapes: sexual ambivalence (frequent in psychosis); homosexual tendencies.
- Overlapping strokes: the writer can dissemble and lie.

- Hooks: diplomacy; hypocrisy; lying; good business acumen.
- Pronounced middle zone: desire for immediate gratification; selfishness.

FERNANDO'S PORTRAIT: He has severe problems with relationships, as evident in his script. His homosexual urges combined with his limited intelligence and intuition push him toward the wrong people, and his attachments are usually excessive. He craves a physical outlet and tries to participate in amateur athletics. Sooner or later Fernando gets kicked off the team because he's made a pass at an unsympathetic teammate.

Fernando's approach to life is very childish. He is constantly entangled in a web of lies and unable to assume any responsibility. He is as well incapable of making the most insignificant decision without seeking the advice of others.

SCHIZOPHRENIA DISORDERS

Schizophrenia strikes 1 in 100 people and varies in its types and its duration, but all are characterized by a loss of contact with reality through grossly irrational thinking and distorted perceptions, such as visual or auditory hallucinations. Schizophrenia reveals itself in disorganized thinking, disturbed perceptions, and inappropriate emotions and behavior. It is always debilitating and may affect its victims sporadically or chronically.

Schizophrenia victims who are induced to paint or draw reveal in detail the terror of their inner instability. Handwriting characteristics are similar to those of any debilitating mental disorder, only more pronounced. For example, the script of the schizophrenia victim becomes either extremely irregular or extremely monotonous. Look for underlined passages and several different styles of script within the very same sample.

* * *

Linda, 46, is not married and has no profession. She suffers from acute schizophrenia and has been in treatment. It is not difficult for you to draw her portrait.

BRIEF ANALYSIS: Linda's script is extremely irregular and shows many sinistrogyric strokes and hooks (past problems which have not been overcome). Angular, tapering strokes (aggression, inner violence; destructive tendencies) accompany strange shapes in the lower loops (vengefulness; frustration of the libido). Note also the arcades (ability to manipulate others; arrogance); heavy punctuation and *i* dots (psychosis); upward-launching endings (temper tantrums; aggression); and altered letters (unreliability).

* * *

Rachel, 18, is a potential student. She lives and travels with her parents and has been in psychoanalysis for many years.

about you over a year ago in
magazine, and I have been
you ever since. When I'r
being ~~ seventeen and in
passed out. Well, I wont
I'll be nineteen, but when
Paris I'll be sure to look

Maybe I'll hunt down F.
drag him over with me —

My love,

Handwriting analysis:

- A very meandering baseline (in spite of the lined paper she uses): emotional instability, moodiness; lack of persistence; lying.
- Irregular, light pressure: poor health and/or weak personality; substance abuse.
- Altered letters: hypocrisy; diplomacy; lying caused by fear and anxiety.

- Heavy *i* dots: mental problems; psychological disorder; unreliability.
- Unfinished letters: inhibition; timidity; anxiety; lying.
- Tapering strokes: destructive tendencies; unreliability.
- Variety of sizes of letters: emotional instability; immaturity.
- Variety of slants: mood swings; emotional instability; mental problems.
- Wide spacing between letters and punctuation marks: schizophrenic tendencies.
- Very large spacing between words: independence; loneliness; lack of communication with other people.
- Fast writing: intelligence; vivacious spirit; impatience.
- Round and angular shapes: maturity; intelligence; analytical and deductive mind.

BRIEF PORTRAIT OF RACHEL: Her aims, actions, and feelings are extremely unstable, and she is often totally disconnected from reality. Her fear of life pushes Rachel into fantasy. Yet she is highly intelligent and has an open, quick mind.

In her anguish she seeks relief in alcohol. Rachel is very independent but lonely. Her mood swings and her destructive tendencies make it difficult for her to finish anything she starts or to make friends.

* * *

Edward, 63, has never worked in any kind of profession. He tried to paint when he was younger. He's spent most of his life in mental institutions and in psychoanalysis.

> Dear George—
> Just a note to let (looking forward to coming Paris next Monday.
>
> Enclosed please find to put up in the store, cor info.
>
> See you then.

Handwriting analysis:

- Childish: immature; poorly developed intellect.
- Round shape: feminine and romantic character; great need for affection; sexual ambivalence.
- Juxtaposed: good intuition; need for independence.
- Limited and tapering end strokes: selfishness; avarice; destructive and psychotic tendencies.
- Capital letters in the middle of words: schizophrenic tendencies.
- Heavy *i* dots: mental disorder; schizophrenia.

- Extremely changing slant: instability; mental problems; moodiness.
- Baseline plunges slightly downward: depression; precarious mental health (in this case).
- Strong, regular pressure: good physical health.
- Signature placed to the left of the message: depressive and self-destructive tendencies.
- Very large, sinistrogyric lower loops: ambivalent libido; this man is not virile; he is sensitive, susceptible, and romantic.

EDWARD'S PORTRAIT: Very unstable and immature in spite of his advanced age, Edward's libido is ambivalent, and he is very selfish and self-centered. He suffers from strong mood swings and feels more and more depressed. He is constantly in treatment and under medication. However, his physical condition is still robust. Most of his personality traits are common to schizophrenia disorders.

*   *   *

Klara, 59, was born in Germany, raised in the United States, and now lives in palatial surroundings near Rome. The only child of rich and well-known parents, she inherited a great fortune. She has suffered spells of schizophrenia since childhood. Her marriage to a Frenchman produced six children, five of whom suffer mental illness to varying degrees.

Klara is alone now. She does not always recognize her children when they come to visit and resists offers of help from a close friend who is a psychiatrist. Though she owns a mansion surrounded by park land, she lives most of the time in a small shack beside the main house and refuses to bathe or to wear decent clothing.

Clearly, reality has no meaning for Klara. Note in the following samples that she mixes the words of four separate languages as she writes. The underlined passages are typical of schizophrenia. Klara's emotions are deviated; her mind completely confused (note the capital letters that appear occasionally in the middle of words). Yet her handwriting also reveals her unhappiness (downward-plunging baseline) as well as her instability.

Klara dwells in a fantasy world, clearly evident in the nine separate signs of lying present in her script (coils, hooks, altered letters, overlapping strokes, a variety of slants and sizes, arcades, heavy punctuation, tapering strokes).

Cara Ingrid e c
Nina bene _ Linda
Arria & family bene
(Alessio ??) Dimitri
Ho trovato Sergio p
tu _ Chissà cosa gli
Io ho già 2 anni ein
Zucht, bin Mitglieder
bin Freundin geworden

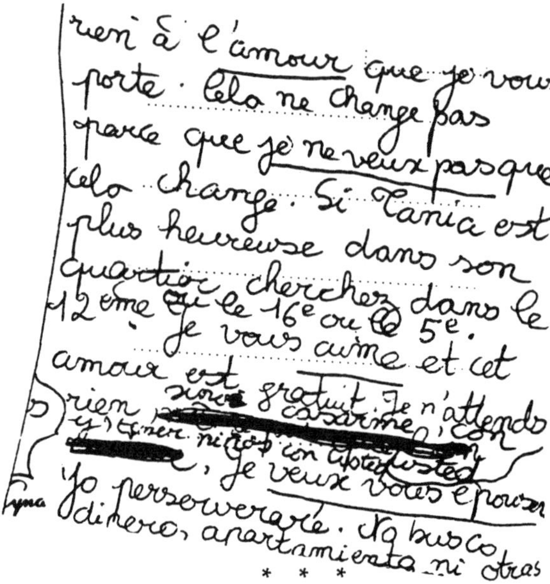
rien à l'amour que je vous
porte. Cela ne change pas
parce que je ne veux pas que
cela change. Si Tania est
plus heureuse dans son
quartier cherchez dans le
12ème ou le 16e ou le 5e.
Je vous aime et cet
amour est gratuit. Je n'attends
rien [redacted] con
[redacted], je veux vous épouser
Yo perseveraré. No busco
dinero, apartamiento ni otras

* * *

Marilyn, 37, has spent many years in a home for the mentally disabled. At present she is an outpatient and lives alone. A nurse and a doctor come to see her regularly. Marilyn received a good general education and is highly intelligent. This is revealed in her small and fast handwriting.

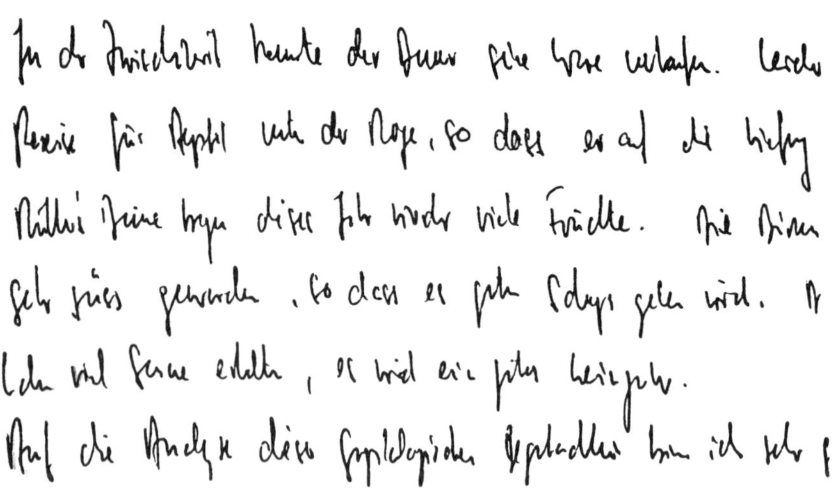

BRIEF ANALYSIS: Marilyn's script is very monotonous, an indication of her schizophrenia. The baseline is extremely meandering, and her letters are altered, with large, irregular spacing. The *i* dots are heavy, and the script is difficult to read. The slant is slightly sinistrogyric, but the pressure is light and regular. Her mental condition is stabilized with medication. Considering her age, there is little hope for curing her mental ailment and changing her into a happy, well-balanced person.

SELFISHNESS

The following samples are included to illustrate the general aspect. See also the close relation to other disturbing personal traits, such as cruelty. The signs to look for include:

• Tapering and sticklike strokes.
• Lack of margins.
• Pronounced middle zone.
• Tight spacing.
• Sinistrogyric, angular strokes and shapes.
• Lack of end strokes: the letters finish abruptly.
• Coils and hooks.
• Overlapping strokes, mainly in vowels.

* * *

Daniel, 33, spent four years in prison for robbery.

BRIEF ANALYSIS: You have by now acquired the ability to see immediately that this man is not very trustworthy. His handwriting is confused, like his mind. It looks tight and is entangled without any end strokes. Daniel is selfish and very greedy. There are high, tapering, and sticklike strokes (cruelty, violence, aggression, destructive tendencies, vanity). The high upper stems show that Daniel's aims and ambitions exceed his potential. There are many hooks and coils (lying, unreliability, selfishness, greed). The covered strokes show that he is capable of lying and dissembling. He does not feel secure. His writing speed is rather slow; he is not very intelligent.

Daniel's script looks tough and aggressive. His willpower is weak, and he needs psychological help, as his mind is extremely confused. His emotions are deviated. He lacks feelings and empathy for other people, and is capable of stealing money from his best friends.

*   *   *

Hendrik, 37, is a decorator.

BRIEF ANALYSIS: His handwriting is extremely large and slow (reduced intelligence and intellectual abilities; immaturity). There are many hooks and coils (selfishness, cupidity, business acumen). Altered letters and heavy *i* dots indicate the writer's anguish. Most vowels are high and narrow (attachment to money; vanity). Entangled lower loops reveal the need for a physical outlet. The very meandering baseline points up his instability. Hendrik suffers from acute psychosis; however he is less violent and aggressive than the antisocial personalities analyzed earlier.

SUBSTANCE ABUSE: A FINAL NOTE

Although drug and alcohol abuse are covered in detail in Chapter 3, on physical illness, it is obvious that mental deterioration must accompany the physical deterioration of addiction. Many people who suffer mentally turn to drugs and/or alcohol initially as a way of easing their inner pain.

Do not dismiss the "self-medicating" aspect of addiction. What begins as a way to feel good can end up as a way of feeling nothing at all.

* * *

Flora, 44, was a heroin addict. She committed suicide within three months of writing the following sample.

BRIEF ANALYSIS: Her handwriting is very angular (cruelty, inner violence); confused; and shows altered letters and a fluctuating slant (emotional instability; mental illness). Numerous tapering strokes reveal her destructive tendencies.

The pressure of her script is irregular and very light. Flora was suffering from a precarious physical and mental state.

* * *

This addict died of an overdose one year after writing the following sample. Was his death intentional? We will never know. Analyze the sample and draw your own conclusions.

5

TESTING YOUR SKILL

Do try not to cheat by looking back through the preceding chapters! Even if you can't help yourself, this exercise will help you strengthen your skills. Most of the test samples have not appeared earlier. Each sample reveals one of the three physical or mental states suggested, among other traits.

* * *

1.
    (a) ☐ good physical and mental health

    (b) ☐ precarious physical and mental health

    (c) ☐ emotional instability

*The publishing wasn't h
promotion would seem
books at poetry conver
and locally. We have
in both England and
sell his poetry here.*

2.

(a) ☐ good mental health

(b) ☐ schizophrenia

(c) ☐ neurotic tendencies

* * *

3.

(a) ☐ alcohol abuse

(b) ☐ drug addiction

(c) ☐ good mental health

* * *

4.
    (a) ☐ precarious physical health

    (b) ☐ neurosis

    (c) ☐ psychosis

would you probably be would oblige.

* * *

5.
    (a) ☐ weak physically; friendly person

    (b) ☐ dynamic, healthy person

    (c) ☐ cruel, violent, aggressive person

man who talks.

* * *

6.

(a) ☐ reactional depression

(b) ☐ psychosis

(c) ☐ schizophrenia

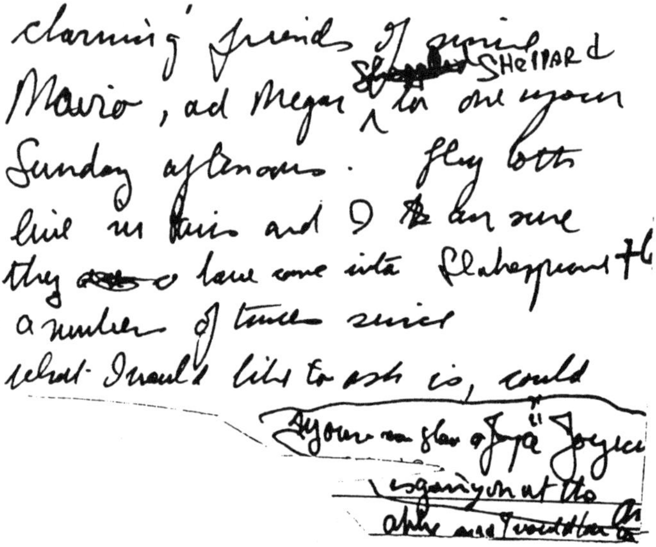

* * *

7.

(a) ☐ precarious mental health

(b) ☐ good physical and mental health

(c) ☐ cardiovascular problems

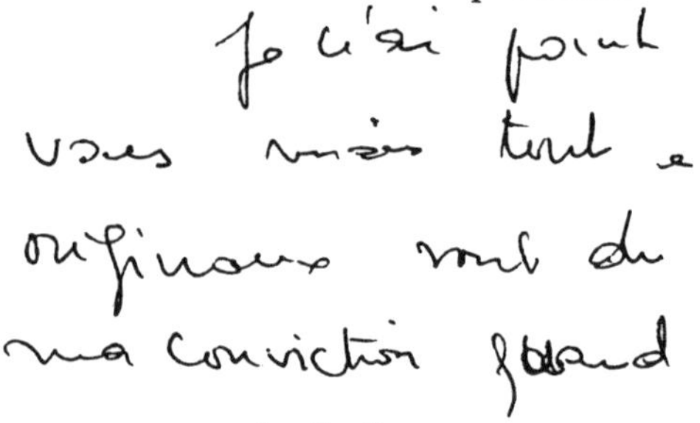

* * *

8.

(a) ☐ normal, strong libido

(b) ☐ living in a fantasy world

(c) ☐ excessive masturbation

Contact"
Radio .
du President Kennedy

* * *

9.

(a) ☐ homosexual tendencies

(b) ☐ regressive libido

(c) ☐ lack of libido

* * *

10.

(a) ☐ destructive tendencies

(b) ☐ schizophrenia

(c) ☐ alcohol abuse

George
Ford
a letter this
That Penguin

* * *

11.

    (a) ☐ good mental health

    (b) ☐ precarious mental health

    (c) ☐ good physical and mental health

Dear Thomas,
Paris is fine and
meeting so unusual
Hope your days in ...
are exceptionally eve

* * *

12.

    (a) ☐ precarious physical health

    (b) ☐ robust health

    (c) ☐ psychosis

London. Lady Mac has
delightful young Australian
with her, no room for me,
has turned out for The

* * *

13.
        (a) ☐ anxiety

        (b) ☐ major depression

        (c) ☐ schizophrenia

*   *   *

14.
        (a) ☐ robust physical and mental health

        (b) ☐ precarious physical mental health

        (c) ☐ cruelty

*   *   *

15.

     (a) ☐ fantasies of violence and debauchery

     (b) ☐ friendly person

     (c) ☐ manic-depressive disorder

e looking. Says the apartment she
he one in which she used to live. The
own. Thinks that either her old boyfriend,
the new lessees said she broke in. Admits
having been evicted. Gary ~~Gil~~ Gilmore had
til recently.

*   *   *

16.

     (a) ☐ physical ailments

     (b) ☐ mental deficiencies

     (c) ☐ well-balanced, healthy person

2 I am an american.
2 minded the store
urf and wot envited
eorges for toast and

*   *   *

17.

(a) ☐ multiple personality

(b) ☐ good mental health

(c) ☐ antisocial personality

cher nani
très bien; ?
baignade. je
émilie Brayon -
Tout va bien
Mes amis sont adorable

* * *

18.

(a) ☐ well-balanced person

(b) ☐ relationship problems

(c) ☐ schizophrenia

John BRAUCHTE UNBEDINGT
hat deshalb mein auto ge
wer weiss wie verkauft. Sei
an all den märchen die dieser
(aus finanziellen Gründen habe ich d
gekämpft um mich zu scheiden. Der u
John scheint so wie der Vater zu sei.
Nun ist die Kummer für den jüngsten Son.
und nun verstehen wir schon etwas. Der junge
ex-Hausmeister von MonteLirete ist ein elender
süchtiger (es gibt viele ÜBERALL) und untersucht
für Räubereien, deswegen wollte er hier
versteckt in dieser Landstrecke leben (mit Frau
und 2 Kinder). Sicher hatte er meinen jüngsten
Sohn lesset "den ...

* * *

19.

            (a) ☐ good health

            (b) ☐ drug addiction

            (c) ☐ alcohol abuse

Monsieur,

suite à notre entretien téléphc
vous confirme par la présent
de la société GOAL SYSTEM

*   *   *

20.

            (a) ☐ reactional depression

            (b) ☐ psychosis

            (c) ☐ schizophrenia

seute une enquête -do
fe -de l'élève -de lyc
-de la réaliser, -des à
un questionnaire. C'es
se à vous afin -de sa
analyser quelques u
et quelles sont nos c
si bien sûr vous cou
*   comptant n*
veuillez agréer, pui
mes meilleurs senti

*   *   *

21.   (a) ☐ schizophrenia

                             (b) ☐ emotional withdrawal

                             (c) ☐ anxiety and
                                     cardiovascular
                                     problems

[handwritten] Alas, nothing came of that
Literary project but from
a novel of my

* * *

22.   (a) ☐ precarious physical
                                     and mental health

                             (b) ☐ robust physical
                                     health

                             (c) ☐ criminal

[handwritten] on the basis that I got to
do his work because he used
e became great friends at what
- me really and another character,
into, to edit this first thing?

* * *

23.
    (a) ☐ major depression
    (b) ☐ poor physical health
    (c) ☐ eating disorder

However I'm enjoying my job, seeing snow for the first extended time, going to learn to ski, white water kayaking later in the spring. Enough.

*   *   *

24.
    (a) ☐ physical ailments
    (b) ☐ mental ailments
    (c) ☐ good health

'I was an independent thinker, & and it was good for me to work. a lot of things if I wanted to! . to me that I would get a job you think is the right there tell me! Now that I'm free Almost every day I meet a girl, her but not more than that handwriting? (See postcard)

*   *   *

25.
      (a) ☐ physical ailments

      (b) ☐ drug addiction

      (c) ☐ alcohol abuse and
           psychotic tendencies

[shorthand notes]

*   *   *

SOLUTIONS

1. (a) Strong, regular pressure; easy-to-read script; regular shapes and spacing; slightly meandering baseline; progressive slant; good disposition of the three zones.
2. (b) Words belonging to different languages; slightly downward plunging baseline; heavy *i* dots; tapering endings; discordant letters and various shapes; irregular pressure.
3. (a) Irregular pressure; clubbed vertical strokes; heavy *i* dots; threadlike and tapering words; difficult-to-read script.
4. (a) Twisted, uncertain strokes; descending baseline; slightly irregular pressure.
5. (c) Angular strokes and hooks; sticklike strokes; heavy, irregular pressure; tapering strokes.
6. (b) Altered, discordant, and forever changing shapes of letters and slant; very meandering and downward plunging baseline; tapering strokes; a great variety of sizes; sinistrogyric strokes.
7. (c) Irregular, light pressure; broken strokes and letters.
8. (c) Numerous coils inside the vowels and inside some other letters; sinistrogyric slant.
9. (b) Weak and thin lower stem.
10. (a) Angular, sinistrogyric, tapering strokes; angular loops.
11. (c) Strong, regular pressure and shapes of letters; progressive slant; ascending baseline.
12. (a) Light, irregular pressure; unfinished strokes and endings.
13. (c) Impossible-to-read script; light, irregular pressure; downward plunging baseline; altered, discordant letters and shapes; underlined words; entangled letters and lines; threadlike words; various sizes.

14. (b) Light, irregular pressure; unfinished and broken strokes; tapering words and strokes; open vowels.
15. (a) Ink-filled letters and vowels; tapering strokes; altered and discordant letters.
16. (c) Regular pressure and shapes; easy-to-read script; regular spacing.
17. (a) Heavy punctuation; two different handwritings; meandering, downward plunging baseline; altered strokes and letters.
18. (c) Tight, monotonous, childish script with many underlined words; altered and overlapping strokes; capitalized words; arcades; some words written in a completely different handwriting.
19. (b) Slow, artificial, slightly regressive script; fluctuating pressure; twisted strokes; capitalized words; childish aspect of the handwriting; arcades in *m*'s and *n*'s.
20. (b) Script of a very monotonous aspect; pasty strokes; ink-filled letters; oval shapes; sinistrogyric lower loops
21. (c) Discordant letters written in a great variety of shapes; extremely meandering baseline; irregular pressure with broken strokes; changing sizes of the letters; difficult-to-read script.
22. (a) Light, irregular pressure; twisted strokes; altered letters; difficult-to-read script; overlapping strokes; changing slant; unfinished letters.
23. (a) Downward plunging baseline; heavy *i* dots; altered letters; overlapping, tapering strokes; wide spacing.
24. (b) Sticklike, sinistrogyric *t* crossings; unfinished, broken strokes; downward plunging baseline; arcades; slightly monotonous aspect; regular, medium pressure (good physical health).
25. (c) Clubbed vertical strokes; irregular pressure; tapering strokes; altered, threadlike letters and words; slightly descending baseline.

SCORING: Give yourself 5 points for each correct answer.

$$125 - 100 = \text{Excellent}$$
$$100 - 75 = \text{Good}$$
$$75 - 50 = \text{Average}$$
$$50 - 0 = \text{Read the book again!}$$

CONCLUSION

You are a novice no longer. Through your efforts you have acquired sufficient expertise to recognize at first glance whether or not any handwriting sample belongs to a person in good physical and mental health. If you detect precarious signals, you can interpret the nature of the writer's physical or mental distress.

Remember always that everyone's handwriting contains an interplay of individual signs. Only in the context of the entire sample can your analysis or interpretation be made. An isolated sign means nothing. Likewise, your interpretation is an opinion, not a fact. As your knowledge continues to grow, your skills will continue to improve.

If two people's handwriting is never identical, their samples can be similar. Where they are, the meaning of the dominant traits will be the same and will be more pronounced in these people than in the population at large.

Real, intimate details about health and well-being are revealed in the script. Mastering my method has taught you that it's entirely possible to distinguish details of character, well-being, and more by learning to analyze handwriting—even if the writer tries to conceal these details!

Your knowledge of graphology can help you to improve your personal relationships and your business relations as well. Keep practicing, and enjoy your new-found skill.

✳   ✳   ✳

ABOUT THE AUTHOR

Claude Santoy, Ph.D., earned her doctorate in Psychology from the Sorbonne. She has performed handwriting analyses for hundreds of personal clients and dozens of major European corporations, and has written a number of books on graphoanalysis, including THE ABC'S OF HANDWRITING ANALYSIS and INTERPRETING YOUR CHILD'S HAND-WRITING AND DRAWING, both published by Paragon House. She lives in Paris with her son.